American Writers Review 2021

Turmoil and Recovery

American Writers Review
2021
Turmoil and Recovery

D Ferrara, Editor
Patricia A. Florio, Founder

American Writers Review   2021
San Fedele Press

D Ferrara, Editor
Patricia A. Florio, Founding Publisher

Front Cover: Breakthrough - Holly Tappen
Back Cover: And They Danced - Carol MacAllister

Special Thanks To the Judges of Our
2021 Writing Contest:

Jean Colonomos

Richard Key

Lenore Hart

Margaret McCaffrey

Patrick O'Neil

Holly Tappen

Contents

TURMOIL AND RECOVERY

For Those Who Made It Through—
And Those Who Did Not

TURMOIL AND RECOVERY

Note From the Team

Yet another difficult year has passed. Most of us were isolated, lonely, and anxious. For some of us, writing, painting, and photography helped make sense of the pandemic. Okay, baking helped, too.

As difficult as surviving the pandemic was, it was made worse by the polarized attitudes of people in the United States and elsewhere. Simple measures to combat the spread of the disease were mocked and attacked. For people (like our editor) who lost family and friends to COVID-19, the politicization of basic precautions felt like an attack, an insult to those who suffered. Others facing conflicting instructions, changing regulation, and lost income, struck out in their helplessness.

For a while, we wondered if we could get another issue together, whether our readers and contributors could find words and images, or if they found them, would they want to share them. We posted our call for submissions, the first with a theme, waited and hoped.

Our contributors came through: we received an enormous number of submissions. With the help of our contest judges, we selected fine writing and images to craft another issue of which we are proud.

Thank you, contributors and readers. We could not have gotten through this without you.

D Ferrara, Editor

Patricia A. Florio, Founding Publisher

Dale Louise, Copy Editor

Tami - D Ferrara

Requiem for Believers
A. Rabaduex
Winner, 2021 Contest

i.

The only colors alive in that February rain were blues,
red stripes, and white stones standing in formation
as I stepped behind horses pulling the cold casket
and I watched his mother watch her son
get a gun salute.
The blasts, like bullets, could not pierce gray
could not break open clouds and let us hear
the sun still shone somewhere that day.

ii.

The sun still shone on you
beat hard on octagon hats and khaki hands
pulling triggers on blistered desert land.
Those days, everything was too hot or too cold
no place was just right to step.
I sat rocking next to our baby's crib
when you called about the IED,
about your favorite troop wanting to patrol
down the dusty village road,
 and your last word to him was *go*

Sand quenched itself with blood
then swallowed part of you, too.
Ordered to stay, I had to tell you
about the way the sky fell on his flag
that day. How I learned the art of watching clouds,
the art of wait.

iii.
Waiting for you to return at 2 a.m.
in a North Carolina parking lot is when I learned
that blacktop breathes out summer sun
in a sticky twilight sigh
and this was how you did it, too –
evicted the light which nourishes in small doses.
It rose from your sand-burned lungs,
scorched pavement over soft spots.

This is how to exhale God – quietly
into the humid space before dawn's clouds
meet pale mourning.

iv.
They buried the boy in Arlington under Angel Moroni,
you buried your bible in dried red sand under spewed Eucharist.

v.
Sometimes when I walk down the road in February rain, I believe
the clouds will part at winter's end. I wait for it. And now you
wait
for nothing.

Our Prime Minister Says the Vaccine Is Not a Silver Bullet
Anne Casey
Winner, 2021 Contest

Primordial monstera fronds list
in the blistering shade, a solitary
kookaburra silent between
the flagging liquidambar
branches scratching at my
lofty perch—even the cicadas'
earlier vigorous castanet stilled
to a relentless dull trill—a scorching
waft occasionally riffling his breast
feathers, downy white

as snow coating the slopes outside
my father's far-off window,
dusting his muddled head; icy sleet
piercing the winter
-pruned olearia where his cherished
blackbirds cluster on better days

and later here, the kookaburra will return
with his one true love and their
burgeoning brood to fill the swaying
evening branches
with their raucous laughter,

my heart rising to meet the updraughts,
torn between émigré anguish
and shimmering hope.

Red Sky Day
Elizabeth Browne
Finalist, 2021 Contest

The sky was the color of parchment, vaguely yellow. I filled my hot water kettle in the kitchen I thought about the hour and how the sunrise changed the color of the world. I had not yet comprehended that something was wrong. I dumped three scoops of coffee into a stainless-steel French press. Outside the window, the sky turned an anemic cantaloupe color. The kettle roared like an approaching train.

I poured the steaming water into the press, then, mesmerized by the swirling foam, stirred the mixture a few times. The kids' voices rose from the play area downstairs, and I willed the coffee to brew faster. Outside, the rows of homes lining the hills in our San Francisco neighborhood looked the same, but the light still had a pre-dawn quality to it, though it was later than that, and the dimness made the familiar view look ominous. The sky had deepened in color. Before I could catch myself, I yelled, "Hey guys, the sky is orange!" Then, knowing I could wait no longer, I pushed down the plunger on the French press.

"What do you mean, orange?" my younger son, Rory, called up the stairs.

"Look outside," I said. I was staring out the window as I said it, the window through which the California sun usually blazed into our kitchen with a brightness that hurt the eyes. I could not see the sun at all.

The kids exclaimed over the sky as I calibrated how much coconut creamer to stir into my coffee. A few years ago, after I complained of digestive problems, my doctor said, at a certain age, we begin to lose the enzymes we need to digest certain foods. Perhaps this was true, and I did feel better after cutting dairy and wheat from my diet, but I resented the automatic response I got every time I went to the doctor with some concern. A quick assessment— mid-40s, mom of two — and the diagnosis was always "middle age."

Rory marched into the kitchen and pointed out the window. "Why is the sky orange?" he demanded.

I took a tentative sip of my coffee and then blew and slurped until I could tolerate gulps. The coffee roared to life inside of me. My brain began to feel clearer, my body less sluggish.

"I'm not sure," I said. "Smoke from the wildfire maybe?" But I had never seen a sky that color from the wildfires that, for the past few autumns, regularly had ravaged vast swaths of land outside of San Francisco. The smoke usually moved in low and gray, swallowing everything, obliterating the skyline and choking the air. It had a smell, of burning trees and brush and roofs and walls, of chemicals from exploding cleaners under sinks, and the melting sludge of children's toys. When the smoke was oppressive and the air quality was considered most unhealthy, the smell seeped into our house. Our windows, like those in most San Francisco homes, were old and drafty and framed in wood that slowly rotted in the fog and ocean air. When I approached them the toxic campfire odor grew stronger. But now, under a reddening sky, I smelled nothing.

My older son Aaron appeared, scanning the kitchen for signs of breakfast.

"Look, the sky is orange!" Rory said.

"It's the apocalypse!" Aaron said in a creepy, low voice. At 12, he had discovered that being melodramatic could elicit laughs.

"What's an apocolips?" Rory said, as he stared open-mouthed out the window. He was 7 and immediately believed anything his older brother suggested. The color of the sky was becoming more intense, as if the atmosphere itself was on fire.

"It's the end of the world! Muhahaha!" Aaron said this in the kind of deep voice used in movie trailers.

Rory narrowed his eyebrows and looked at me for an explanation.

"This is not the end of the world," I said, and sat down at the table.

"Well, what is it?" Rory asked.

"I don't know," I said, and took a long swig of my coffee.

The local news revealed San Francisco's ubiquitous late summer fog had pushed the wildfire smoke high into the atmosphere overnight, forming a thick layer between us and the sun and blocking out light and heat. I thought about the dinosaurs, and how they might have gone extinct because a meteor crashed to earth and the debris from the impact blocked the sun's rays. Who were the dinosaurs now?

After breakfast, the sky grew darker and redder. My husband Billy went to work at a desk in our bedroom. The kids tackled school via iPads, and I stared outside. Normally this was when I tried to write, but instead I took pictures on my phone and shared them. This was a localized Bay Area phenomenon and social media revealed a prevalent sense of anxiety and an inability to concentrate. The light inside our house, or lack of it, was not unlike the light of dusk, perhaps that of a winter's early evening in a place that was used to snow. But it was now late morning in mid-September in a place blessed with a Mediterranean climate. I thought about a midday solar eclipse I'd witnessed during my senior year of college some 25 years earlier. How the light waned and shadows grew crescent-shaped and my friends and I delighted in dancing in the half-light and taking pictures. In the sanguine darkness of my kitchen now, I did not feel like dancing.

My sons were each in different rooms, staring at screens where their classmates were replicated in little rectangles and their teachers' torsos explained the day's learning topic. I needed to walk the dog, and before I left, I brought the kids plastic cups filled with cheddar Goldfish crackers. Rory gave me a quick glance as I set the snack down. Aaron barely looked away from his screen as he grabbed Goldfish and stuffed them in his mouth. The kids weren't supposed to eat while "in class" but giving them snacks made me feel useful. It was a motherly contrast to the lack of human contact. I could remind them of the world outside of their rectangles, even if that world was on fire.

Outside, ash rained down, but the air quality was surprisingly good. The particulates that could get into your lungs and make you sick seemed absent. I had to wear a cloth mask anyway; it was mandated because of the pandemic. We had, over the past few years of frequent, terrible wildfires, taken to wearing N95 masks to protect our lungs when the smoke was at its worst. My husband's company had given them out to its employees, and we'd bought child-sized masks for the kids. When wildfire smoke smothered the city, those particulates irritated our throats, made our noses run, and our eyes burn. Aaron and I often developed persistent coughs despite the heavy-duty masks and the air purifiers that we ran constantly in the house.

The smoke-fog layer was an effective heat blocker. It had been warm in the preceding days, but now I shivered in my down coat. The cold felt sinister and unfamiliar, not like winter weather, which blew at you from someplace closer and recognizable and smelled of snow.

My dog, an elderly terrier mix, appeared unaffected by the red sky, the midday darkness, and the cold as we wandered to the closest park. He sniffed at succulents and wagged his tail at a passing puppy. The park was on a hill in the middle of the city and offered a sweeping view of the skyscrapers downtown, Mt. Sutro, the city's famous hills, and the Bay with Oakland beyond.

Now five photographers stood behind tripods at the park's summit and a few more onlookers had gathered. We all wore masks. No one spoke. When I joined them at the top and faced downtown, I could not quell my anxiety. The whole of the sky was the color of the last vermillion glow of a sunset. The lights were on in the vacant office buildings downtown. It was dark enough for lights to be on all over the city, and seeing that, seeing all of us, working, learning, cooking, praying and playing under this red, burning sky, frightened me. Then, too, there was something about the group of us, all San Franciscans, all gathered in this hilltop park at the same time, sharing the same anxiety-inducing hellscape, and yet from our silent, socially distanced spacing, not sharing anything at all.

I stopped on the way home and looped the dog's leash around my wrist so I could take a photo with my phone. It was a shot of the road ahead, homes on the hillside, telephone wires crisscrossing the sky. The street was empty of cars and people. This was common now, to be out at midday and see no one on the sidewalk. But the lack of movement, combined with the eerie noontime darkness, the cold, and the strange sky— the photo felt like an acknowledgement of a boundless threat and my immense, unavoidable helplessness.

In the last block of my walk, my fingers began to tingle. My body had warmed, despite the chill. There are easy, judge-a-book-by-its-cover diagnoses: The sky is choked with smoke from a wildfire. You're just middle aged. But more complex diagnoses emerge if you examine patterns over time. Tingling, digestive problems, and muscle issues were symptoms not of middle age but, it eventually turned out, multiple sclerosis. A blaring red sky that darkened even noontime reflected a wildfire and the unusual behavior of smoke when it met fog, but also years of drought and unusually high temperatures; climate change that we'd done little about.

Back in the house, Aaron had finished classes for the morning and was wandering around the kitchen peering into cabinets and opening the refrigerator. "Can I have lunch?" he asked.

Rory was in the dining room adjacent, headphones covering his ears like muffs, his brow furrowed. Every so often he mumbled an indistinct word in Spanish. He was struggling to learn the language via a screen. I tried to be quiet so as not to disturb him and slid some leftover pasta into the microwave.

We kept the kids inside that day. As a parent, my impulse is to protect them and comfort them. But how do you parent in the face of multiple catastrophes? Did it matter what the diagnosis was, if a cure was elusive?

We have tried to keep things normal. But already "normal" feels like something in the past we may never get back. What is normal when the sky is red? Both my husband and I felt unsettled and couldn't keep our anxiety hidden. I kept taking pictures out the window, and then cleaning or cooking out of some instinctual need to create safety and comfort. Billy emerged repeatedly from the bedroom to talk about how unnatural the sky was and how he couldn't concentrate in the dim light when it was actually midday. Aaron and Rory participated in their Zoom classes, ate snacks, and played with Lego bricks. But every so often they would stop to tell me how they couldn't believe how dark the sky was, and how red.

At lunchtime that day after I walked the dog, Aaron stood at the window, silhouetted by the eerie red light. "This is crazy," he said. His voice was no longer full of pre-teen bravado. It was quieter, full of wonder, maybe, or fear.

I slid his bowl of steaming pasta on the table for lunch. It was the only thing I could do.

Moon Gate - Carol MacAllister

Therapy
Sheree La Puma
Finalist, 2021 Contest

A window with a sheet attached.

Breath.
Intimate.
I have a secret
white and dirty. How
I marvel at the weight of words.
A man sleeps on an island, not a king
but a gatekeeper. Long ago, Mars was wet.
This is a parking lot revelation. The hardest part,
wanting to believe the crossings-out, those
scribbled inscriptions. The preacher
with his muddled hallelujahs
praying for God to loosen
my tongue or alight
me with flame.

I admired his precision.
    the blurred margins.

  Sacrifice as an act of love
But what of the sins—opened, read,

and returned to the envelope? I
remember weeping on the steps
of Joe's apartment, the new
grass, slick. I am eight
when I discovered it,
a book, children,
on top the kitchen table,   images ##
  fouling the room
like something dead.

I avert my eyes from the ones groped
or beaten. Disintegration begins at
the folds. A good girl might plant
her boot upon a granddad's head
but I fall asleep in a ritual of
grief that survives
childhood.

Decades
  later someone is digging
a hole. Ready to be planted, I have
  an unencumbered view of the world.
It calls to me
to suffer, just a little longer.
  The night turns blue, the
color of rapture. It enters through the upstairs
        room to rest next to Father.

Poets, come out of your closets
A. Rabaduex

after Lawrence Ferlinghetti's "Populist Manifesto"

Tell us how profane years are over
and what shape was the shadow of the smoke.
Is it ever really finished? – this digging
these shovels hitting stone when we seek a soft bed.
Awaken words that sleep in your cheek,
spit them out like dormant seeds ripe for planting.
Show us the way sounds spill like souls from hospital wards.
Rip off the mask and remind us what is a face.
Because now we look at teeth touching, meditating
on a *sh* and we hear death waiting
like a flick of the fire's tongue.
Moths explode in the woodstove
and schoolbooks are closed
and new babies don't know
that strangers can smile.
The distance from ear to ear
from here to here
from tomorrow to yesterday
has never seemed so far.
Even in our dreams we long for sleep
lavender shrugs at the breeze

we can't smell the time of year
and the sky hangs too low
Clouds move faster than February
carry last year, lost places, forgotten days
and we numb our eyes here.
So all of you sick of the slush,
all you addicted to semantic satiation,
all you who want to see alive the poetic lines
of your grandfather's face,
all you whose voice drowns under pleated waves
of sickly pastel polyester veils
all you who want to fling open your doors and roar—
free the speak easy drunk in your lungs,
all you who've heard the beat of the raven's nevermore—
remove the long, dark visage and breathe.
All you poets, you mind sailors—
anchor your ships in the harbor
take your place in the village square
because we need you to tell us
we need you to say
to say it out of your closets
to say it with your lips
in the open air.

Leave It To Grandma
Gregory Fletcher

The doorbell rang in the middle of supper. In 1964, it was the father's job to answer the door; mothers only answered the phone. Dad yelled, "Linda, call the fire department!" My older brother—by two years, one month, and fifteen days—rushed to the window in the front room. I was seconds behind him. We flattened our faces against the glass, peering off to the right at the faded green 1952 Plymouth Sedan—with fluttering flames in the backseat!

Dad ran our way at the window, frantically searching behind the bushes. "Where's the hose!" Then he took off around the corner of the house. Tom rushed to the back window, and I followed. Dad pulled the hose in, stretched out across the backyard. One arm over the next, back and forth, once he had the nozzle in hand, he darted through the house. "Turn it on," he yelled to Mom as she hung up from the fire department. But when it stretched to its limit, his instruction changed. "Unscrew it!"

By the time Mom had rushed through with the other end, and reconnected it to the front faucet, she looked to the burning car and simply said, "Oh, Joe." The entire car was engulfed in flames.

The fire truck had arrived, the siren had silenced, the neighbors had gathered to watch the flames distinguished, and, still, Tom and I were pressed against the window, not missing a moment. Two hands slapped the glass in front of our faces, and my brother and I jumped back in fright. The dirty hands belonged to the boy next door—Eddie, eight years old. He had a smirk on his face, as if he knew we weren't allowed outside.

When Mom checked on us, I asked, "Why does Eddie get to talk to the firemen but not us?"

"Because he was the one who reported the fire," Mom said. "Such a good boy."

I thought to disagree, but it wasn't the time for a debate. Eddie knew how to charm my mom, I'll give him that. But it was all fake like Eddie Haskell from *Leave it to Beaver*.

The next day, I found more cigarette butts in the backyard than usual. An odd find since neither of my parents smoked. Six in all!

"Hey," a voice said. I looked around but didn't see anyone. "Play with these," the voice added, and a handful of wooden kitchen matches rained down on top of me. I looked up in the tree that hung over the fence, separating the backyards. Eddie!

The backdoor to his house swung open, and his stooped-over grandfather yelled, "Someone's here for ya." He climbed down and rushed inside. From in-between the houses, I saw a Fire Chief's car in the driveway.

Shortly after, my dad's mom from New York arrived for a visit—the first time I could remember. The only thing I knew about her was that she was divorced and lived alone. So my mom had mentioned to her friends. "How sad it must be, all alone at her age."

When Grandma's yellow cab pulled up to the house, I greeted her with a hug—the squishiest one I'd ever felt in my entire life. The first thing to pop out of my mouth was, "I never rode in a taxi."

"Well, we'll have to fix that, won't we." Then she whispered to Mom, "Was it Eddie? Did they prove it?"

Mom pursed her lips. Not a word about it.

Till Dad spoke his mind at the dinner table. "The kid's an arsonist hoodlum."

"But was it proven?" Grandma asked.

"They found enough wooden matches in the garage to light up the entire block. The boy's father is God knows where; his mother works three jobs. The only one to look after him is his decrepit grandfather."

Mom cleared her throat and the discussion immediately stopped. How she could end a conversation without saying a word truly blew my mind.

The next morning, Grandma suggested we take a walk. Mom stayed home to pick up the scattered trash that mysteriously appeared in our backyard from time to time. Grandma told me to lead the way.

"Where to?"

"How about to your favorite neighborhood spot."

That was a no-brainer. 7/Eleven! I explained that it opened at seven in the morning and closed at eleven at night. The name was pure genius. And, equally impressive, it had the longest candy aisle I'd ever seen in my entire life.

Grandma said I could pick three things. I chose grape-flavored wax lips, a box of Hot Tamales, and the candy necklace. I felt sorry for my brother, missing out on this trip. But that's kindergarten—the good and the bad.

That afternoon, Grandma and I were in the backyard on the swing set when the back gate next door opened and slammed shut. Eddie climbed his usual tree and disappeared high up.

Grandma whispered, "Is that Eddie?"

I nodded.

From a pocket, she took out an unopened package of SweeTarts. "You want to give these to him?"

No way, I thought. I'd rather eat them myself.

"Go on. You know how to share, don't you?"

I moped over to the fence and held it up. "Want 'em?"

Eddie looked down and sneered. "Your leftovers? What do you take me for?"

"We bought them especially for you," Grandma said, joining me at my side. "Now get down here and say thank you."

Eddie climbed down the tree and approached the chain-link fence. He reached for them tentatively, as if I might pull them away. But when he had them in his hand, his eyes softened. "Thank you."

"I'm Greg's grandmother from New York. Do you have a grandma?"

He shook his head.

I thought to myself, How could he not have a grandmother? I had two.

"You can call me Grandma if you want," she said. "Or Mrs. Fletcher. Or Margaret. Or Maggie. I even have friends who call me Sally. Take your pick."

So many names, I was speechless. I knew for a fact her full name was Margaret Raphael Fletcher. Why on Earth would anyone call her Maggie or Sally?

"I'm taking the boys downtown tomorrow," she told Eddie. "You're welcomed to join us if it's okay with your folks. What time does school let out?"

"Three o'clock."

"Perfect," she said, placing a hand on my shoulder. "Let's see if your mother needs any help."

Eddie stood there watching us go inside. I'd never seen that surprised look on his face before.

The next afternoon, a yellow taxi pulled up in front of the house. Tom, Eddie, and I rode in the back seat. Grandma sat in the front with the driver. They talked and laughed all the way downtown like best friends.

The cab stopped at the new courthouse, across from where President Kennedy had been shot the year before. Inside, Grandma led us into a courtroom where we sat in the last row—a wooden pew, similar to the ones at Irwindell Methodist church, minus the slots for hymnals. A jury entered in a line, just like a church choir, but without the matching robes. The judge sat in the pulpit and read from a piece of paper that was passed to him from the jury. "Guilty."

A man stood at a front table, and was led out a side door. Then the congregation dispersed without the judge walking down the center aisle to greet us at the main entrance.

Instead of leaving, Grandma moved upfront to a uniformed officer. Then beckoned for us. She introduced us to Officer O'Leary who led us out the side door into a small windowless room. The only furniture consisted of one wooden chair against the wall. He told Eddie to lift it. When he tried, the chair wouldn't budge. It was attached to the floor. "Take a seat," he added. "It's not very comfortable, is it? Anyone who breaks the law ends up here. How'd you like to spend your days in a small, cramped room like this?"

Not me, I thought. No windows, sunlight, or fresh air.

O'Leary asked if we had any questions, but I could only think of one: Why were we here? Then he escorted us to the main hallway, shook our hands really hard, and made us promise never to see him again. "Kiss the Blarney Stone for me, Mother."

And even stranger, Grandma agreed.

Outside, she said with delight, "Wasn't that fun?" She seemed elated as if getting off a ride at Six Flags Over Texas.

We walked past many stores, one after another. I'd never seen so many, side by side. But not one 7/Eleven in sight.

We came to a trailer parked on the side of the street. Army recruitment posters were plastered on the outside: "Uncle Sam Wants You!" and "Be a Man Among Men." To my surprise, Grandma led us inside and introduced us to a soldier who greeted us. After a private conversation, he beckoned for Tom and Eddie to sit with him at a desk and handed them each a color brochure. He explained it was too early to sign up for service, but added, "Keep us in mind, ya hear?" He shook their hands and approached Grandma. "A pleasure, ma'am." He thrusted his stiff hand up to his forehead, and Grandma returned the salute. It was very impressive.

On the street, Tom asked if Grandma expected him to join the army. She looked more to Eddie than to Tom. "If you want to travel the world for free, it's good to know your options, don't ya think? Not to mention a paycheck and a college education."

Next, Grandma led us into a hospital where she talked to someone behind a counter. We were directed to an elevator and up five floors, where a nurse greeted us. We followed her along a squeaky-clean hallway to a room with a skinny, old man in bed. In order for him to speak, he had to cover the opening of a tube sticking out of his throat. Worse yet, his voice was scary raspy, and he was missing most of his teeth. The few he had were brown, my least favorite color. Grandma nodded, as if she understood every word he said. But not Tom or Eddie. Their eyebrows were higher than I'd ever seen before.

Grandma shook the patient's hand, and a tear ran down his face. She motioned for us to shake his bony hand with dark veins. Dad had always prepped me for strong handshakes: "Show him what you've got; squeeze his hand like a man." But I thought it best to match his limp grip and forego any sign of manhood.

After Tom and Eddie shook his hand, the nurse led us out, and said, "I hope ya'll come back real soon." I'm not sure we felt the same way. She and Grandma hugged like old friends.

Downstairs, Grandma couldn't find the exit and asked a janitor to point the way. When she made him laugh, he leaned his mop against the wall and escorted us all the way to the street. The more they talked, the more they laughed. He waved goodbye and said, "Sister, you're about the nicest Yankee I ever did meet."

When Tom finally spoke, he asked if the skinny man in bed was dying.

Grandma nodded.

Eddie asked, "From what?"

"From cigarettes." Then she stepped into the street to hail a cab.

A pedestrian asked, "Where're ya'll from? Taxis don't get hailed in Dallas." He pointed to an empty taxi stand where we walked to, and waited. No bench. I was tired and wanted to sit down.

"You've got a private chair," Grandma said. I looked around but didn't see one. "Feet apart," she continued. "Toes pointing out." We did as instructed. "Bend your legs and squat down. Good. Now, rest your arms over your knees."

Hmph. It was comfier than expected.

When a taxi finally arrived, we jumped in the back seat again, and Grandma in the front. "I-35 to Oak Cliff," she said.

When the cab stopped, it was a dream come true. Kip's Big Boy! We walked inside, and Eddie whispered to Grandma, "I don't have any money."

Shadows of COVID - Katie Toskaner
Finalist, 2021 Contest

"My treat," she said. And what a treat it was: hamburger, fries, Dr. Pepper, and a hot fudge sundae! We all agreed, it was the best dinner of our entire life.

At home, Mom and Dad were out. Eddie waited with us on the front porch. "How much family you got?" he asked.

"Most everyone I meet."

"Don't it take blood to be related?" he added.

She shook her head. "Extended family. And now, you're extended family, too. Which means we look after each other, do nice things, help each other out. The more family you got, guess what?"

We chimed in unison: "What?"

"Life is sweet."

Grandma was anything but alone. She had friends and family wherever she went. With taxi drivers, courthouse officers, soldiers, nurses, patients, janitors, and waitresses.

Dad drove up in the new white Valiant, and Mom yelled out the window, "We left the front door unlocked."

Dad yelled in a playful manner, "Why not tell the whole neighborhood?" He stuck his head out the window. "Did everyone hear? The house is unlocked and opened."

Mom laughed while Dad parked the car in the driveway; though, I wasn't sure what was so funny. But I found it so interesting when her laughter brought about tears. And sometimes, running to the bathroom.

Eddie got up to leave. "Thanks, Grandma," he said. She pointed to her cheek and turned her face. He bent down and kissed her. Then he passed my parents in the driveway. "Goodnight Mr. and Mrs. Fletcher."

Mom and Dad looked in complete shock. Grandma shrugged. Her eyes sparkled as she smiled. From that night on, we never had cigarette butts or trash in the backyard again. And matches and fires were a thing of the past.

. After Tom and Eddie shook his hand, Grandma led us out. The nurse waved, and said, "I hope ya'll come back real soon." I'm not sure we felt the same way. She and Grandma hugged like old friends.

Downstairs, Grandma couldn't find the exit and asked a janitor to point the way. When she made him laugh, he leaned his mop against the wall and escorted us all the way to the street. The more they talked, the more they laughed. He waved goodbye and said, "Sister, you're about the nicest Yankee I ever did meet."

When Tom finally spoke, he asked if the skinny man in bed was dying.

Grandma nodded.

Eddie asked, "From what?"

"From cigarettes," she said. Then she stepped into the street to hail a cab.

A pedestrian asked, "Where're ya'll from? Taxis don't get hailed in Dallas." He pointed to an empty taxi stand where we walked to, and waited. No bench. I was tired and wanted to sit down.

"You've got a private chair," Grandma said. I looked around but didn't see one. "Feet apart," she continued. "Toes pointing out." We did as instructed. "Bend your legs and squat down. Good. Now, rest your arms over your knees."

Hmph. It was comfier than expected.

When a taxi finally arrived, we jumped in the back seat again, and Grandma in the front. "I-35 to Oak Cliff," she said.

When the cab stopped, it was a dream come true. Kip's Big Boy! We walked inside, and Eddie whispered to Grandma, "I don't have any money."

"My treat," she said. And what a treat it was: hamburger, fries, Dr. Pepper, and a hot fudge sundae! Eddie said it was the best dinner of his entire life. Tom and I agreed.

At home, Eddie waited with us on the front porch. Mom and Dad were out. I realized Grandma was anything but alone. She seemed to have friends wherever she went. With taxi drivers, nurses, patients, even the courthouse officer called her "Mother," and the janitor called her "Sister."

"How much family you got?" Eddie asked.

"Most everyone I meet," she said.

"Don't it take blood to be related?" he added.

She shook her head. "Extended family. And now, you're extended family, too. Which means we look after each other, do nice things, help each other out. The more family you got, guess what?"

We chimed in unison: "What?"

"Life is sweet."

Dad drove up in the new white Valiant, and Mom yelled out the window, "We left the front door unlocked."

Dad yelled in a playful manner, "Why not tell the whole neighborhood?" He stuck his head out the window. "Did everyone hear? We left the front door open. The front door is open."

They laughed while Dad parked the car in the driveway. I wasn't sure what was so funny, but I laughed anyway.

Eddie got up to leave. "Thanks, Grandma," he said. She pointed to her cheek and turned her face. He bent down and kissed her. Then he passed my parents in the driveway. "Goodnight Mr. and Mrs. Fletcher."

Mom and Dad looked in complete shock. Grandma shrugged. Her eyes sparkled as she smiled. From that night on, we never had cigarette butts or trash in the backyard again. And matches and fires were a thing of the past.

Photograph - Jeff Talarigo

Some days you're the seed, some days the bird
Anne Casey

Through the gaps in the fence, I'm watching a wattlebird
bronco-riding a long, bobbing stem—so absorbed
in plucking plump rapture from the dark crimson heart
it's oblivious to the buck and weave, purple floral spikes
brushing its scarlet cheeks like some portent
from a forgotten fairy tale, essential ingredient
in a witch's secret scheme.

Weeds thrive beyond the palings,
the grass thigh-high in places,
another sign of the times—
like the boarded-up shops
(one on our corner
shuttered suddenly yesterday
after twenty-five years),
the half-empty city streets.

A shard of sun catches a dragonfly's rise
over the fence. I saw some bush bees

there the other day——
the first in years since
the now-disappeared
council worker mowed
their cluster of wind-seeded crocus.

There are moments I'm consumed
by the jolt
of how our world has veered,
others bewitched by the hum
of wildness
overcoming concrete.

Coastal descant
Anne Casey

Four hours north
of our new normal, a daily changing
tableau—already elsewhere from
the chatter and chant of ascending scales
in LA, London, Brazil; a sinkhole in Italy; a landslide in Java;
a plane fallen from the sky; wreckage
of the assault on democracy in DC—
we have hurtled out of city snarls
through Eucalypt forests shooting
new green across the blackened scarline
of last summer's megafires, past vast shocks
of long-legged birds wading near wallowing gums,
their mottled trunks drowning in this year's floods,
to breathe again

clear air carrying a tincture of salt,
a trace of coastal rosemary,
count blessings falling like soft rain
on my longed-for west-of-Ireland heathers
and here, on spiring cordylines, Norfolk Island pines

scraping a last skirmish of downy clouds,
their slender cones far below snagging
olive chains of Neptune's necklace
along the snaking tideline,

a sea eagle gliding high
over sands fringed in the wild fleshiness
of samphire, and higher over lobelia blooms
purple-tonguing rain-swollen air; where
Blue Triangles flit between the fresh dazzle
of Golden Guinea flowers twisting
past ragged Elephant Ears
sagging in steamy Strangler Fig shade,
Fishbone Ferns filigreeing
the drifting sea breeze——

here where banksia trees turn into wind
off churning surf, their gnarled arms
spreadeagled into brine-laden sky,
contorting around rock, a symphony
of seed pods parrots a lorikeet's
brief speech, and a psalm of
cicadas echoes
wave-song.

The startling grace
of a rainbow's full cascade
into cobalt ocean
over a horizon thirteen thousand
miles from my home coast,
yet so uncannily alike;
a ghost crab dances *en pointe*

across our scarecrow shadows
before we swelter uphill
again through saltbush,
a cuckoo mocking
our blundering
passage

as three hundred metres below,
the small blot of a lone swimmer
sinks beneath the glistening surface—
a cormorant racing
its own shadow
over his
wake.

Lisa - D Ferrara

The Kind of Asian I Am
Lynnette Li

"What kind?"

The elderly man spots me the moment I step through the locker room doors onto the pool deck. He soaks in the hot tub, a towel draped around his neck, the ends dipping into the bubbling water. I want to pull the towel out and ring it dry.

He nods at me and I nod back. Do I know him? In this small Chicago neighborhood, the answer is often yes. But no, I do not. He is Caucasian, white hair. He smiles at me and I smile back because that is what I do when an older person smiles at me. My nod might even look a little like a bow and I hate that it looks like a bow, but forgive myself because that is also something I do: I bow to older people.

I unwrap my towel from around my chest and hang it over a bar along the wall.

I've only been to this pool once before. The water is too cold but resolutions and a desire to get cardio that is also low-impact outweighs my preference for warmer water. And afterwards there is that hot whirlpool to look forward to. I feel the man's eyes follow me. A tingle of self-consciousness prickles my skin: the cold of the water startles my foot as I test it.

I jump. I always jump. I am not an inch-by-inch-wade-in-slowly kind. I am a plunge-and-then-deal-with-the-jellyfish-later kind.

I'm done swimming but must not have been in the pool for long. The man is still in the hot tub. I'm winded and I feel like my body has worked hard and I am ready for that hot water. He seems friendly, but I am looking forward to sitting alone, savoring, breathing, easing in—oh, yes, easing into that hot water—that's an exception to the thing I said earlier about being the jumping kind. I DO ease into water when it is hot. I am the kind who relishes the scalding rings climbing up my legs, past my knees and thighs, until they join together at my hips. Then that single ring around my body climbs higher and higher past my waist and breasts until it is a hot ring around my neck, the steam obscuring my face.

I swim eight more lengths, alternating between breast and backstroke. Eight more lengths, then I know I am done. He is climbing out of the hot tub now, holding that sopping wet towel dripping at his waist. His skin is pink down to his toes. Bright red shorts cling to his hips and thighs. I smile through chattering teeth as I walk toward the tub. He steps sideways blocking my path.

"What kind of Asian are you?" His head tilts to the side, a look of awe and curiosity wash over his face.

This is an old conversation—the script is curled at the edges, over-rehearsed. I am not overcome by the same sort of incredulity and rage that friends say they experience in this moment. I have a face that says, *talk to me, ask me how to get to the corner of such and such place, ask me what kind of Asian I am.*

I want to ease into that hot water. I also do not know how to be unkind to an older person.

"Oh, well..." and the familiar feeling of wanting to share the real true answer that is too long for the space between the pool and hot tub spreads over my chest. *Just give the simple census answer Lynnette,* a voice inside me says, its lips turning blue.

"I'm... well, three of my grandparents were born in China, but they..."

"Ah, yes! Ni Hao," the man says with slow exaggerated tones, bowing slightly.

When I hear Mandarin, my back straightens. Perhaps it is because I know just enough that if it were truly necessary and helpful, I could use it. But it is not a language I grew up speaking. I imagine it's the same feeling someone who took French in high school has when visiting Montreal twenty years after graduating. My brain knows I don't need Mandarin now, but my body reacts and I inhabit a posture of ultimate politeness.

"Or should I say, *Neih Hou*?"

I recognize the Cantonese because lots of the early Chinese immigrants at my church in Detroit growing up were from Hong Kong.

It is not that I am not annoyed. I am. I simply do not have it in my body, in my words, in the processing from my brain, to my breath, to my tongue, to my mouth, to say so aloud.

My eyes glide over the sun spots covering his forearms, to the wrinkles in his skin gathering near his elbow. I am the kind of Asian who wonders what it would be like to pinch him there— whether it would feel fleshy and full, or thin and papery—whether I could pull it and how far the skin would stretch. I am the kind of Asian who wonders what it would be like to pull the skin until it stretches long and far, and then like releasing a rubber band, fling the man along with his soaking wet towel into the cold lap pool. I wonder if he would squeal *Eeeeeeeeeeee!*

I am the kind of Asian who flips through old yearbooks from elementary school. The pages, in black and white, are printed on plain non-glossy paper, and filled with fading faces of blond-haired, blue-eyed Polish Catholic kids. My thick black bob with bangs straight across framing round black eyes, make a saturated ink stamp in a single rectangle in the center of the rows of kids in Miss Wetmore's PM Kindergarten class.

Smiling very well, my mom shakes her head with pride, *you were always very good at smiling*.

I am the kind of Asian who kisses the trumpet player at a party after our big spring jazz concert in college. The kind who kisses him hard because his lips are full and something about how quickly I know they need to vibrate to blow into that trumpet is sexy to me. I'm the kind who has too much to drink sometimes, whose face doesn't flush, so it is hard to tell. The kind who hears people murmur *Jungle Fever* as I kiss the trumpet player because he is black and because seeing us kissing on a sofa at a college in Kalamazoo twenty years ago is new, unusual, novel.

"But I'm not white," whispers the kind of Asian I am. I'm the kind who wakes up the next day and cannot remember last night. The kind who feels my body aching in places I don't remember using.

When he calls, he is sweet. I listen for clues about last night. His words sound like care and respect and solidarity, we're in this together, aren't we? We know what it's like to be different, to be minorities.

"I've never dated a girl like you."

I'm the kind of Asian that doesn't remember last night, but forgives him. He announces to the entire brass and rhythm sections,"I had Chinese take-out last night, if you know what I mean."

They know exactly what he means and give him big jovial slaps on the back. I'm the kind of Asian who goes out with him anyway, who might still want to kiss him.

Who is also angry at him but does not tell him.

I'm the kind of Asian who laughs lightly and bows while saying "Ni Hao" to the elderly man by the pool. I move toward the wall to retrieve my towel. He reaches out to me, grabs my arm between my shoulder and my elbow, and folds me into his warm wet pink body.

"I'm so proud of you," he says patting my back. "It takes a lot for you to be here."

I am the kind of Asian who nods slightly to the elderly man as I back away toward the locker room without my towel while saying thank you. I am the kind of Asian to be proud of.

Photograph - Patrick O'Neil

It's a Free Country
Patricia Dutt

Millie and Wayne met in the basement of 518 Seneca Street just over a year ago in early January when snow was crusty, and the virus was in China, nowhere else.

"Hey Freckles! Mind if I sit here?"

A lean handsome guy, with a recent haircut and unblemished jeans, loomed over Millie, grinning. He wore a green plaid shirt that smelled new and made his eyes iridescent.

"Be my guest," Millie said, and she shuffled the metal chair over an inch, making room for him. A host of other replies came to her mind: "Sure!" or "If you dare!" or "It's a free country, buster!" but in many ways, she did not believe it was a free country. Those with money made the rules and enforced them. And if you were black or a minority, forget it: justice was a pie in the sky that you barely saw before it disappeared into someone else's kitchen. Wayne also believed that the country was not free, but more fervently.

That night at 518, Millie was celebrating a year of sobriety, and she felt ready to share. She wasn't a gabber, she was a *this is where I am, straight-forward person*, and *here's a sense* of *where I will go*. Wayne picked up on her energy and asked her out for coffee, and one thing led to another and before she realized it, she had moved out of her sober house and into his apartment. The apartment was out in the country over a garage, and it was cold and the carpet was old, but it had been two years since she'd slept with anyone. Millie held onto Wayne's wrist all night long and felt his warm body besides hers. It was the most wonderful night of the past ten years of her life.

Next came the discovery phase. They found out they wore double socks in winter and their favorite dish was black beans with tomatoes, garlic, and cumin, with melted cheese on top—you were in heaven. Millie was also a self-help devotee: Dr. Ruth, yoga with Adrienne, Dr. Weil, Medium, podcasts, meditation. Wayne associated self-help with subservience and a lack of independence. And because Millie's brain was functioning better—she'd guess at about 80 percent—she started reading again.

"Why are you always reading?" Wayne said one night after dinner. They both cleaned up together, another plus in Millie's mind.

"How are you supposed to know about the world if you don't read?" Millie noticed when she moved in that Wayne had no books—except for a dictionary because he was an obsessive on-line Scrabble player. Not even one paperback mystery, and she'd always assumed everyone loved a good murder story.

"What's the point? Everything important comes over the internet."

"The information is different," Millie said. "It's digested. Reflected and organized. And if the book is a novel, well most of the time, you can't help but develop compassion for the protagonist. You know—the leading character?"

Wayne grunted, and returned to his computer where he spent a lot of time. He had over a thousand Facebook friends—so he told Millie. Millie guessed it was because of his friendly demeanor. Facebook was just one more obligation, so Millie had no presence in that fiber optic realm. Still they cooked dinner together, cleaned together and slept together. Then most mornings Millie drove off in her used Hyundai to a retirement community where she was a companion to an elderly woman named Naomi. Naomi and Millie played cards and watched TV. Millie taught Naomi yoga breathing, and then Millie sat spellbound as Naomi related her adventures and close encounters that she and her sister (the rest of the family gone, murdered) had had with the Nazis. Naomi had a tattoo, but it wasn't the conventional tattoo that the in-crowd championed.

Millie did not know what Wayne did for a living. He was on his cell a lot, and always printing off documents, and recently maps, using Millie's printer. He went through reams of paper. Maybe he was a salesman or a lawyer? She heard the words *sue* and *lawsuit* and *legal*. Or maybe he sold real estate? Even a drug dealer, she thought, noting the bolted steel locker in the garage. So what? No one was perfect, least of all Millie.

One night, about ten months into their relationship, as they sat around the rickety kitchen table, ambient temperature of 62 degrees, Wayne said: "Promise you'll never leave me."

Millie almost said, *Till death do us part*, but something stopped her. "Why would I want to leave you?" she said.

After that she started coming home from work in a quiet way, so you could not discern her footsteps ascending the outdoor wood stairway. It was not uncommon to hear Wayne on his cell, agitated, as if someone had taken his parking spot, or exultant from winning at some kind of game. One morning on her way to work she almost backed over Wayne's hunting gear. Since November, he'd spent Wednesdays at the shooting range, all day, then on Saturdays he hunted. He must have been tired because he always tucked his guns and affiliated regalia away in the metal locker. As she moved his stuff, she noticed an American flag. What the hell, she thought, staring at it. Three stars?

Then Wayne had stopped calling her *Freckles*. That in itself wasn't a deal breaker; the deal-breaker would have been if he'd said: "No more *Omms* here."

Millie meditated every single morning, a 35-minute kriya mediation. She sat on the couch, turned on her app, and did ujjayi pranayama, bhastrika, the three omms, circle breathing, then for the last ten minutes laid down and fell into a deep meditative state. It was in this state that her inner-therapist emerged.

"You think something's going on."

"Yes."

"You need to trust your intuition."

"My intuition says to leave."

"Well?"

"I made a promise."

"So?"

"I don't want to be a promise breaker."

"Hmmmm let's see. Did you ever promise to return a phone call, and not return it?"

"At one time in my life I made lots of promises."

"Look, Millie, let's cut to the straight: change is the way of the world. Climate changes, your neighbors change, you change the sheets on your bed. What's the difference?"

"I don't know."

"People change all the time."

"But if I break one promise, then I start breaking more, and before you know it, I'm drinking again."

"That's just plain stupid."

"It is?"

"Don't just sit there, Millie. Don't be a fool. Find the evidence."

It was January again, also the night of the decisive Scrabble Tournament. They'd each won four games, and tonight's winner would buy takeout, winner's choice of restaurant. Little did Wayne know that Millie had been generating lists of Z- and Qu-words using his dictionary. Not only that, but during the tournament, she managed to occupy every single red, triple-word square. Half of the time when she put down her letters, he said: "You just took my move!" She considered taking the move back, but she earned it. Equal rights for women: it was her own #MeToo moment. And her last word, using all seven letters, she played on Wayne's N. The word was S-E-D-I-T-I-O-N. That extra 50 points did it. And it would have been okay if Wayne had pouted, violating one of the *Eight Characteristics of Emotionally Intelligent People*. Instead, he flung the Scrabble board so hard against the wall that the board ripped. Then he took his computer into the bedroom and closed the door and slept by himself.

Millie just sat there, meditation having trained her not to react, but to pause. Breathe. Maybe he was anxious about his hunting trip? He was leaving tomorrow. Good he was going, she thought, let him cool down.

The next day was Wednesday, the day that Millie stayed until 9 pm at the retirement community. After dinner, Millie and Naomi were watching TV, and they saw the footage of the mob violently attacking the Capitol. The mob had spears, weapons, brightly-colored hats and flags. One flag had three stars on it.

"Breaking the glass," Naomi said, looking sadly at Millie. "That's how it started. Kristallnacht. 1938."

When Millie got home, she threw clothes and books into the two suitcases that she owned. She left behind some belongings, and a note telling Wayne her Mom was sick (she was). Millie did not say she would return, because that would be lying, and lying would set her back. To her, truth was a matter of life and death.

Her mind was working right up there at 95 percent. It would be foolish to say she would not miss Wayne's company, the comfort and economic security, and she wasn't sure where she was going, but she knew for sure, she would find a place.

IF (Barbie discovers that Ken is a Proud Boy)
Anita S. Pulier
Finalist, 2021 Contest

If you were nearsighted
I would buy you glasses
to sit on your nose

If you were deaf
I would place small hearing aids
deep inside your canals

We would dance together
you would allow me to see myself in
your beautiful face

but it is not your eyes blinding you
or your ears deafening the cacophony
it is your untouchable, unreachable mind

and I am unable to translate
from the sidelines, drowning in love
while watching you ride the swells of hate.

Photograph - David R. Brubaker

Fear of Flying
Jennifer Lagier
Finalist, 2021 Contest

For weeks, a pair of swallows
guard their nest, hidden under foxgloves
in a whiskey barrel planter.

First, four tiny speckled eggs,
then miniscule hatchlings appear.
Beaks gaping wide, they chirp to be fed.

Today the first fledgling tests his wings,
clumsily careens over backyard fence,
crash lands on the curb bordering driveway.

My heart nearly stops, breath catches
as I consider fragile baby bird,
threat potential of cats, dogs, people.

Avian parents stand guard,
click frantic warnings until the little one
flutters back to protected sanctuary.

During pandemic summer,
I isolate within home or garden walls,
shelter from what kills, keep myself safe

In This House
Lois Perch Villemaire

I've grown older in this house
these many burdensome months,
turning on lights,
taking care on stairs,
moments of lightheadedness,
vision changes,
not recognizing hands with age spots,
reluctant to take walks, it's
too cold, windy, or wet.

I've grown older in this house,
intimate with every corner and surface,
knowing where and when sunlight appears,
spilling across polished wood floors,
revealing hair and dust particles.
Frequently wandering to windows,
raising and lowering shades,
like sending signals somewhere,
to mark beginning and end of day.

I've grown older in this house,
noticing the clock has accelerated,
daylight fleeting, as dusk creeps in,
inviting deer to appear.
Evening dominates,
recalling grandiose intentions,
lost, forgotten, overshadowed
by distractions, futile wishes,
isolation, and regrets.

Soon
DeWitt Clinton
Finalist, 2021 Contest

These are the last days, or at least
We suspect so, as all have passed
Through another distilled moment,
Though how many more do we have
As that's not clear to any of us, but
Think about it for a moment, please
As soon, perhaps not so soon, we'll
Not have any more time, and who here,
Or you, just glancing at this, doesn't
Want more of that, but then, some of us
Are so beyond our expiration date,
So we'd hope they'll go quickly, but
Not in any queue, and certainly not
At the same morgue, or whatever
Last cold bed might be waiting, but
Then as for the rest of us, we'll all
Have to wait our turn, won't we, and
Of course some want to completely
Ignore what's just around the corner,
And others have seen a hearse appear

Over and over either in their dreams
Alone at night, or just slipping into
Daydreams if anyone has time for
That sort of play, but so many of us
Just don't know, do we? And none
Of us look forward to that time, but
For many, it's been quite wonderful,
Yet for others it's a long nightmare
And who'd want that forever and
Ever for so brief a time here, where
We are, and as well, where we're not.

Tearing Down the Wall
Mona D. Miller
Finalist, 2021 Contest

Hunkered down at home during the pandemic, we started to see our house differently. Every spot that needed to be repainted, reupholstered, or redone was calling out to us. Somehow, we'd been able to avoid this for years. Of course, during most of those years we weren't home 24/7 and we often returned from work when it was dark, and not easy to see anything, even if we had been looking. Now, our 2400 square foot world was the only one we saw. It clearly needed some work.

Our daughter's bedroom showed signs of ancient water damage, with ripples and cracks in the paint. She was now 32, married for five years and living in San Francisco. The leaks had been fixed long ago, not that you would know from the waves and huge cracks in the paint. It was time to have the room repainted. But that meant that we would have to take down an enormous collage that she had created between ages 13 and 17.

Photographs, magazine covers, newspaper clippings, bits of posters, and other writings and drawings spread across two walls, one behind the white desk and the other the adjacent wall it met at the corner. From a distance, this messy accumulation looked like black mold. Everything was taped to everything else, and applied to the wall with tape.

At one glance I knew I would not be able to save it. There were stories about Arlo Guthrie and John Lennon. There was a *New York Times Magazine* cover with a Pop Art look (a silly, radially symmetric design in bright colors, with lots of yellow), a reproduction of the famous kiss photographed in the 1940s by Robert Doisneau, and lots of portraits of Black jazz musicians, including Duke Ellington. I didn't recognize all their names. Kurt Vonnegut (my daughter's favorite writer) appeared several times, both old and young. In between the clippings, the magazine art, and reproductions of record covers, were snapshots my daughter had taken of her face, often when she was lying in bed, as well as pictures of her feet. Newspaper pictures of Betty Friedan and Gloria Steinem were on the walls, too.

Near one snapshot of herself was an index card where she had handwritten, "the portrait of the artist as a young woman." As I took it down, piece by piece, I realized that the placement of these images and pieces of writing was not random. The self-portrait snapshots were carefully placed. Her gaze was almost dreamlike, simultaneously sleepy and intense, large, deep green eyes (like my mother's) waking up and just beginning to discover something. It all had some kind of order. And it was deliberate and self-conscious.

How could I not have seen that? I suppose I had allowed her bedroom to be her sanctuary, but I was often in that room, especially for the first ten years of her life. (I don't remember when bedtime stories stopped, but they were a nightly ritual. She often made me make them up, which was exhausting.) The expanding wall of images and text started later.

She was growing very fast during those years, becoming quite tall. I wondered if her feet seemed a little farther away every day. Maybe that was what had led her to take pictures of one foot. Probably she was just lying in bed, or on top of it, thinking, and felt like taking a picture of her foot at that moment. So she did.

Her interests were far-ranging. One article on the wall was about a designer of leather chairs. The chairs looked like tote bags for a body or stylish tan leather fortune cookies into which one could tuck oneself. It was the fascinating collection of a fascinating, complex girl. There she was, scrolled out over time on the walls, manifesting so many different interests. I was surprised to see so much evidence of my own influence. I hadn't expected to find Betty Friedan, Gloria Steinem, or Robert Doisneau, but there they were.

It was quite painful to take it all down. The act of tearing down the wall brought home to me, quite literally, that she didn't live with us anymore, that she was no longer my child but a grown woman, and that I did not have a visual guide growing before my eyes to all the things that interested her. The contents of the collage were so old that the papers crumbled in my hand. I took video of the wall and also lots of pictures, but the room would never be the same. Now, the freshly painted white walls showed off the dormer window centered under the gable, and the interesting angles on the ceiling, due to the gable. More than half the room had a normal flat ceiling, while the part near the window sloped lower.

We took down the warped frames that contained colorful Disney cartoon cels (Aladdin and Jasmine from Aladdin, and a skinny, evil-looking but well-dressed sorcerer from a very old Disney film). The newly painted room looked very fresh, almost nautical, especially without the filthy Roman shade that our daughter and various babysitters had touched and made dirty. (I kept telling them not to, but it never worked.) It did not look like a teenage-girl's room any more. As we wait for a new shade, the room is especially bright, flooded with sunlight, exposed. The white walls are bare.

I had not meant to excise her from the room, which we still called "her" room, but a kind of deep split had happened. I found it upsetting. Of course, she wasn't gone from our lives, and we still had all our memories of the years she had lived at home, but the raw physical evidence of her presence, her creative self, her warm, sweet, messy, lively, expansive energy, was gone. (She naturally smells like vanilla.) I tore down all those pictures and clippings and snapshots—with her permission. She was a loving, compassionate and understanding person. She knew we needed to get that room (now our guest room, often for her and her husband) into shape. She asked me to take a video, which I did.

My mother would never have let me decorate my room like that. Certainly an ever-expanding, Scotch-taped barrage of material, often at angles sloping upwards, would never have been allowed. I wouldn't even have asked. It was not a matter of whether we owned where we lived or rented. After the apartment that we rented in New York became a co-op and my parents bought it, I had little choice in the look of my bedroom. My mother selected the furniture, the bedspreads for the two twin beds and the curtains. She picked the artwork, too, some of which I loved and have to this day. (I'm particularly fond of a print of a young girl with chin length blond hair in a late nineteenth century green and white vertically striped dress with a big bustle, looking serious and a bit concerned, carrying her little red purse. Standing in front of a tall red chest, she is just on the threshold of something.)

I didn't want and never liked the solid gold bedspreads in a matte material that looked like heavy silk but wasn't. I didn't mind the furniture, but I wouldn't have chosen it. My mother even kept some of her books in the bookcases in my room. She was interested in paranormal psychology, metaphysics, Edgar Casey, and astrology. When my friends came over, they teased me about "my" choice of books.

I had a different relationship with my own mother than with my daughter. I think the depth of both relationships is the same, but its expression was not. My mother was born in Poland in 1915; I was born in Coral Gables, Florida, in 1953. My daughter was born in Los Angeles in 1988. My mother was an immigrant who arrived in the United States at age 7, in 1922, not knowing a word of English. She started her life in America on the Lower East Side in New York. She worked in her parents' grocery stores through her teens. In the very early days in this country, she had to take baths in a pickle barrel in the kitchen of their apartment, something she despised.

As her parents' fortunes gradually grew through unceasing hard work, including the work of the three children, my mother, the eldest child, threw herself into schoolwork and academic achievement. She graduated from high school at 16; from Hunter College at 20, in 1935. She went on to a PhD program in psychology, then a relatively young field. Marriage in 1939 to my father, a doctor, American-born, but first generation, interrupted the PhD study. She ended up with "only" a Master's in psychology.

In contrast, I was born into relative affluence, the youngest of four children. The first two, my older sisters, were born at the beginning of World War II, in 1942 and 1943. The third child, my brother, was born in 1946, almost nine months to the day after my father got home from the war. Then there was me, born in 1953, the "baby of the family." My mother made it very clear that no-one was allowed to call me that or to treat me like that. Of course, every stranger, on meeting our family, referred to me that way.

For a trained psychologist, my mother had some interesting ways of being a mother. We lived in a very small town in Central Florida for two years before we moved to New York. Mother had flown up to New York, found us a place to live in Manhattan, and returned. I asked her what color our new house would be. She thought about it, and said "I think it's brown." Brown sounded ugly to my nine-year-old ears. What she had forgotten to tell me was that we were moving to a seventeen-story apartment building. I'd hardly ever been in an elevator in my life at the time—our new abode had a doorman, and three separate banks of elevators. Our new home was on the 11th floor. I soon learned I could not bounce a ball on the floor for fun at night after we moved. The transition from Cocoa Beach to Manhattan was a shock.

Like my daughter had, I started writing creatively as soon as I learned to write. I was always busy writing plays, stories, skits, or poems. My mother always wanted me to be a writer. Unfortunately, when I lived at home for a year after college, trying, unsuccessfully to find my way into television or film production, her way of encouraging me was to suggest that I "Sit down and write a masterpiece." Those familiar with paralyzing self-criticism will recognize that this is not helpful.

When I was in fifth or sixth grade, my mother managed to compete successfully against people two decades younger who'd just gotten out of graduate school on an exam given by the New York City Bureau of Child Guidance. She started working full-time as a school psychologist then. She loved working. I was very proud of her, but I also missed having her at home when I came home for lunch, or immediately after school.

Would I ever make my daughter cry every week when we spoke on the phone from opposite coasts? (My daughter did live for five years in New York while we were, as always, in Los Angeles.) I used to cry after dutifully spending an hour on the phone with my mother every Sunday.

I made a conscious choice never to be as critical with my daughter as my mother had been with me. I wanted to maintain very high standards of conduct, but I also wanted my daughter to feel strong, confident and at ease with herself. My daughter made it easy. She was independent from the very beginning. She strode into pre-school at age two and a half—they took her early, even though she wasn't completely toilet trained—and left me, practically weeping, in the parking lot. "Bye, Mom," she said, and was off.

Mothering is an intimate relationship, but it is also one that is played out in public. Mothers take their children places, they drop them off and pick them up, they handle their children alone and in the presence of others. When children misbehave in public, usually their mothers deal with them. When they are very little, the mothers dress the children; their influence may continue for years. My mother was still telling me to change my clothes when I was 35 years old, and I did as I was told. She was usually quite right, not that that made it any easier to take. I remember my husband looking on in amazement as I just accepted her decision and put on a different blouse and pair of slacks for a family event.

My husband's parents and my parents were from different generations —I was the youngest of four, with older parents, and he was the oldest of five with a mother who was only 20 when he was born. My oldest sister, the one born in 1942, was only 8 years younger than my mother-in-law. She could have been the mother of my youngest brother-in-law, who was born 24 years later. I found it deeply gratifying to be the oldest kid in my husband's family—his younger siblings actually listened to me!

As a child, I'd been surrounded by people who always did everything better than I could, and who seemed to know anything that I might want to point out to them already. I was in a terrific hurry to grow up and be able to do everything the rest of them could. To my young self, it seemed that my mother thought that being "immature" was the worst thing you could be.

It felt deeply gratifying to see signs of my influence on the wall, and to see how profoundly engaged my my daughter was in music, in writing, in the arts. Bob Dylan was everywhere. Andy Warhol was up there, too. In addition to loving the pop music of her own day, our daughter had become quite an authority on Classic Rock, which her father and I loved. She could always "name that tune" in a note or two.

Classic movies from the 1950s, including Rebel Without a Cause, took up part of the wall. A young, cinched-waisted Natalie Wood looked out just as the drag racing cars had taken off.

As each new interest or passion arose, I investigated it; I often found them quite interesting. Probably in connection with her loving the works of Lloyd Alexander and Welsh mythology, she became fascinated with the lute. That led me to embark on a wonderful (albeit unsuccessful) adventure to find her a lute teacher. In turn, through a delightful, charming lutenist who was then a leader of the ensemble, Musica Angelica, I found a lute repair guy. He lived in his fascinating studio in Orange County, with wooden instrument frames on the walls, like unfinished bodies. (The lutenist warned me it would take a while to get my daughter's lute back—the repair guy functioned on "Renaissance time.") My daughter sent me on a series of creative adventures, as I tried to support her interests. She deepened my world. She filled it with love.

While I tore down a physical wall, there is no wall in the love between us. That was probably true of my love for my mother and hers for me; it just hurt a lot more, at times. As my father told me, "your mother is a very dutiful woman." She had her rules and her standards. I do too, but I hold the reins over myself and my daughter more loosely.

what is a dream after all
Mary K O'Melveny

what is a dream after all
something that comforts in the night
or frightens us awake
trembling—or in tears of terror

maybe it's a bird
soaring south over checkered corn
lime green grasses silken soybeans
riding wind columns
like a hobo on the rails

or is a dream a voice
that coaxes us toward safety
or refuge
or escape
or a long walk through arid deserts
clutching a rosary
and a half-empty bottle of stale water

maybe a dream can walk
out of a convenience store

light up a new cigarette
joke with friends
drive home listening to
Ain't Nobody's Business

maybe a dream
is louder than we think
maybe it could
wake up a crowd
shake up the lies they've fashioned
take them to a place of compassion

imagine how a dream might swim across a river
and emerge clean and rested and whole
on the other side   safe in a parent's arms
ready for a new life

maybe a dream puts on a yellow coat
stands in chilled sunlight
turns us into believers

Hope In The Unseen
Mary K O'Melveny

The Perseverance Rover carries a plaque
honoring health-care workers who have
battled COVID-19. Even though no one
is there to read it, the gesture seems right.
We who have huddled in our homes or
shelters hoping to escape viral assaults
need a positive focus after a year of
navigating fears as raw as pocked,
rock-rimmed craters. The Red Planet
has hovered above us all our lives,
offering avenues of escape, wanderlust
and wonder. Now, more than ever,
we want to emerge from isolation to
something larger than our pandemic-ridden
life stories. What better way to escape
than to ride along with science toys
as they tumble down toward ancient
riverbeds and dust-filled caverns?

To join the search as they scour beneath
crust and cracked soil in search of lessons
from once-lonely beings who may have
harbored their own hopes for deliverance.

Shacharit
Mary K O'Melveny

According to Jewish law, the earliest time to recite the morning service is when there is enough natural light "one can see a familiar acquaintance six feet away." Among the blessings offered are prayers for healing, compassion, peace, wisdom and forgiveness. The time for morning services ends at astronomical noon referred to as *chatzot.* On May 27, 2020, the US death toll from COVID-19 passed 100,000. By mid-February 2021, it had passed 500,000.

Let us pretend the sun is rising,
that it is time for morning prayer.
We are sorrow's congregants, aware
of fate. Our desire for love is tantalizing.

Our daily losses are agonizing.
We've begged for endings to this nightmare.
No one disputes that its toll is unfair.
Endless numbers are demoralizing.

Six feet apart we stand. Polarizing
grief has propelled us here

to watch as light emerges, sheer
as a silk shroud, mesmerizing

each mourner. Our need is not surprising.
We bow before a new day, stare
as night's rough edges disappear.
Such devotion should be energizing

yet we remain somber, apologizing
for our failures of faith. We're
humble in supplication, laid bare
as newborns. Moralizing

does not become us. Theorizing
proves of little aid to cures. Where
is the balm of solace? Can there
be healing without compromising

stains of regret? We're realizing
patience might prove useful. Is God there
if we stay fervent, turn away threadbare
promises, abandon patronizing

pleas for forgiveness? As we're sizing
up our chances at redemption, beware
the great temptation to ensnare
victory in defeat's jaws. Sermonizing

is not our strength. Advertising
mercy does not grant it nor ease despair
when, despite our pleas, it fails to appear.
We want resurrection. Souls reprising.

Let us pretend the sun is rising.
Too soon the time for morning prayer
will pass. As congregants, we need to share
our pain. To find love galvanizing.

Stop - Rachel Elam
Finalist, 2021 Contest

The Excavator
Dawn Denham

I had what I wanted. It's not that I didn't at any fixed time. Or never did. I'm studying artifacts—journals, letters, photographs—to get the record right.

I wanted to teach. I taught. I wanted to write, and so began the slow walk toward myself, fraught with self-doubt and criticism, and I wrote. I grew.

Once, my new husband and I said we wanted to travel the country in a Volkswagen Vanagon. We bought an old but hardly used Westfalia the color of burnt orange, though officially it was described as tan. It was closer to rust. A thin layer of plastic film still covering the unused mini-fridge and stove burners. We traveled across the country from Connecticut to California, north on Route 1A to Astoria, Oregon, then east along the Columbia River Gorge. Down into Colorado on our way to the desert, Tucson, where we'd live for six years.

We hiked in the Catalinas, discussing how we would deal with sexism once we started raising babies. We had one baby, a boy, who changed everything. We dreamed of returning to New England one day, of restoring an old house somewhere near the ocean. We left Tucson in segments: First my husband for his new job in Architecture, and then our boy and I, after I passed my thesis exams. We arrived on the Seacoast of New Hampshire in pieces, but we'd done what we'd said we wanted to do: Travel, school, jobs, house, child. Miles in our bones.

I have done a hard and some may say foolish thing, opening these old journals, going all the way back there to write a love story with a sad ending. I have returned to my 24-year-old self on the cusp of marriage and a new life. I wasn't finished with the previous life. I wasn't finished.

Two months ago, I started with our photographs, loose in boxes and organized in albums. Our lives together in Kodacolor affixed to long white pages under flimsy clear sleeves made from a plastic I later learn breaks down. Polyvinyl chloride or PVC known as vinyl (what records of made of) is unstable. We thought we were preserving our life between the faux leather covers, but PVC releases a gas that over time corrodes history. My written words, then, maybe the only reliable account. What has time done to them?

I reached for the 30 or so journals because I thought what I read there could deepen the memories I've been shaping into paragraphs about the end of this long marriage. I thought going back would help me describe what I saw and felt and thought then. What I thought then—at 24, 25, 26, 30, 36—was unfortunate and sad, and today, I think as I read, what a colossal expenditure of energy, gut, and heart. Page after page, year after year, the litanies of indecision, uncertainty, questioning. My desperate need to understand who I was, what to do with my life, what I wanted. Nail it down. I could never feel good about myself or anything I did or was doing. I had no faith, no ability to trust, no belief. I'm exhausted reading her, this young woman processing, distilling every little thought, reaction, occurrence to make meaning of her daily life—What time has done to me. My ability to want was always present. My ability to manifest was also always present, but these pages attest to a crippling self-doubt, self-criticism, and depression. I lived in stasis. Paralysis. I could not see that wanting, reaching, and achieving is living and an eternal process; I could not see that I was doing it all just fine.

I've stayed on my couch most of today. I've watched three movies as I drifted in and out of sleep: a historical romance between two women, a thriller, and a British chick flick. My part-Maine coon Archie draped across my belly, my Goldendoodle puppy Abbie at my side. I know that I'm processing what I'm reading in my journals. It's gestation, and I require rest, but knowing this doesn't stop the critical, shaming voice from repeating: You'll never finish your book.

It's nearly sunset when I jump up, slip on my old Dansko clogs, a pair of thick garden gloves, reach for Abbie's leash and walk her out my front door. The sky-blue house I rented four years ago in north central Mississippi sits high on a hill above Wagner Street and Water Valley's Main Street one block to the west. I've avoided the bank of wide, crude cement steps laid into the steep hill rising to my Egyptian blue wraparound porch. Since I've moved in, the cement steps have remained caked with light tan and reddish mud, leaves, weeds, and sticks. I'm ready to clear it all away.

I arrived here with years' experience clearing, planting, trimming, raking, thinning our gardens and yards surrounding our former New Hampshire home. Here, I decided when I moved in, my hard work would be done inside and in front of a computer. But the mud rises, and now that my lovely beau Eddie and I have trimmed the fig trees flanking the steps, I want to clear the space for the days when we will harvest the small, purplish, soft fruit.

Standing below and facing the top step, I drive the small square shovel Eddie loaned me under the hardened mud, pushing with one foot again and again until it cracks and falls free. I scoop up chunks of dirt, leaves and weeds and toss the clumps to one side. I hold the nozzle-less mouth of an old hose over the cleared area, stopping to sweep away debris and water with a plastic broom I keep on the porch. There are 12 steps. One at a time.

Abbie leaps and runs and inserts herself into the small mounds growing along both sides of the steps. I have to tie her to the porch where she sits alert and barking. It seems no matter what I do, the lack of drainage will remain a problem. Water begins to lay in the corners; perhaps the angles are off. I can't completely clear the hose water from each step. I fear rainwater will always pull soil from under the white and scraggly but tenacious crabgrass at the top of the steps down to the corners where it will thicken into mud; stuck. This water, this dirt, this Mississippi will win.

By the time I get to the bottom steps, my clogs are soaked. My linen jumper, also soaked and mud-spattered. Sweat drips generously from my brow, down my cheeks and plops onto the ground. I climb to the top, take off my gloves and hold my thumb tightly across the hose mouth, trying to create enough pressure for a forceful spray. Waterfalls form down both sides of the steps; brown water reaches the landing—a large slab of cement and begins to rise where weeds and wide swaths of more crabgrass form a natural dam. There is nowhere for the detritus to go. Now I understand why the dirt dries and cakes here, too. I bend and glove-less push a smaller shovel under the soggy patches to loosen the weeds' hold. Then I pull, tearing off large pallets which I sling over my shoulder. My hands are the brown of the water; I wonder at insects but keep shoving the small tool under the weeds. I unearth two whole sections of concrete walkway I didn't know was there; the brown water continues to swirl and move like a river.

My ex-husband the architect used to say, "Water always wins." I cut small wedges into the mud beyond the cement slabs, encouraging the water to flow into the grass. Water wins, but I will give it way.

I wonder what I look like. Sweat and grime and mud now caked on my jumper legs, my ankles, my clogs, my face, splattered. I am breathing hard and remind myself to engage my core with every move; this work is exercise. I will need to borrow Eddie's wheelbarrow, too, and a wide rake, his hose with the fancy nozzle which will surely push the last of the mud from the concrete.

It's a little after six. I'm supposed to have dinner with Eddie and now I'm going to be late. I'm extremely agitated by Abbie's nonstop barking. I roughly walk her to my bedroom door at the end of the porch, push off my clogs and push her inside. I enter and take off all my clothes at the door; it's a short walk to the shower. I don't want to track in mud.

I'm thinking I'll text Eddie to tell him I'll be a little late. I'll wash my hair even though I washed it the day before. But I'm standing in the shower with a head full of suds and I'm sobbing. The mud has tracked me inside. All of it. I bow my head and let the grief come.

I understand that working hard and full out in this yard is a trigger. Because this is how I worked on the property of the home we once made in New Hampshire. Inside and out. This is what I did for six, seven hours a day, breaking ground, digging up roots, planting and moving, thinning, and spreading. I built gardens, planted trees, laid walkways, cut edges, and spread mounds of mulch. I painted porches and trim and lay stones. There was a time when I answered that wanting, to make gardens. Here in Mississippi, I had no desire to touch or mold this earth, in part because of my disdain for the place my parents had chosen for their retirement. For 20 years I'd kept this Mississippi at a distance whenever I visited. Bu once I chose it, I began to acknowledge its beauty, content to accept whatever appeared and with gratitude.

Now, I am pulled to this ground. Within weeks, I'll begin to dig and plant, weed, and thin branches, claim this acre. To allow mud and grime and sweat and stones now means what, that I have let go? That I know I want to stay here?

Because once upon a time, we'd said we wanted a home, to restore an old house, to give a sacred place to a growing son. We said we wanted to landscape and create pockets for sitting and socializing and dreaming. I remembered wanting then, all the way back then when my boy was four, five, six, seven, to watch him grow past the sunflowers we planted by seed together, past the arch we built over the garden gate. And then, more. To welcome him home during college breaks and meet his friends. To meet the young woman he loves. To attend their wedding and one day welcome their own babies. His father and I in that old house that our bodies had restored, standing in the doorway, greeting them all. The two of us making coffee in the kitchen. Wrapping presents on Christmas eve after sending them all to bed. A home, safe harbor, landing strip, as our miracle of a boy began his own swirling. That was what I'd dreamed of and said I wanted. In the shower, clear water streaming down my shaking body, I thought of all that will not bloom for the three of us now. What I was once again saying goodbye to as the mud slipped through the drain.

Once I believed I did not know what I wanted. I did not have what I wanted. The self-loathing for unfinished things. For not doing when it seemed everyone else was. The shoulds. The comparisons. The wasted hours. I lived in a tightly woven trap of self-sabotage. It was steel and it was air. Year after year, those words. A whole life lived through the lens of worthlessness and self-doubt. There's a reason why I cut that Ziggy cartoon from a newspaper in which the round-faced boy/man stands at one end of the long, horizontal box, facing forward, looking up hopefully, his butterfly net slung over his shoulder, not registering that directly behind him hovered a mass of butterflies, filling the rest of the box just behind and beyond his arcing body.

I am excavator, a person who removes earth carefully and systematically from an archaeological site in order to find buried remains. The turned and tainted narrative about not knowing became my root and anchor. Stubborn like crabgrass. Willful like water.

And let's be real: I'm still asking the same questions. Who am I, what do I want, what am I supposed to be doing with my life now? A middle-aged and divorced woman starting again? It's frightening to recognize that maybe I am still that shattered, adrift, unsure young woman who let a young man save her again and again, who wanted love to be all. When I tell Eddie that I am still asking the same questions, he says, "Hooray!" as if to say, "This is how to live a life!" But I shudder. Because somewhere along the way, deciphering and naming want became an exercise in attaining a fixed thing. Success is achieving it. Asking the same questions now assumes I've never had what I wanted or that I still don't know what I want. But I do. I did. I am the same—I am made of all this—and I am not the same. I am fluid. I can tell the difference between the sentences then and the sentences now. I'm that close.

"My growth has come out of ruin," writes Ekua Hagan about Gina Frangello's *Blow Your House Down*. And why wouldn't mine? Ruin breaks everything down. Everything broken down— if left long enough where it fell apart—fully decays. Returns to a former state. This mulch, this humus, deep and pungent and damp, will make other things grow.

My ex-husband and I never had the conversation where we asked, "What happened to us?" It was a sudden and violent cleaving. Silence is safest now. But as I read my journals, stare at pictures, write to understand what happened to us, I know the story of my marriage is really the story of broken me trying to become more fully human. I know what happened to me. We are all of us just trying to figure out who we are.

The Tricksters
Peter David Goodwin

How do they do it?
A marble, hidden under three walnut shells
with movements slow and graceful
as he moves the shells around his temporary table
and we watch, watch the shell
that hides the bright marble
his patter is smooth, teasing, challenging
as he displays the marble
hides the marble
moves the shells, just three
three identical shells
and one hidden marble
see the marble, watch the marble
see, here is the marble
where is the marble?
For a ten spot, I'll give you a twenty
for a twenty I'll give you double
look no tricks, no sleeves
just my fingers in motion
moving slowly, hypnotically
yet the marble remains hidden

and we, the curious observers
the challengers, the educated
are mystified, frustrated, and poorer.
We drift away, as another curious crowd gathers...
it's a skill, a skill that can be learned
I could learn it, you could learn it
anybody can learn such a skill
and not just by tough, tattooed, T shirted
smooth street talkers
its a skill we can all play
and many of us do
wearing suits, ties, and respectability
looking a little over fed
but then its called
not three-card monte
but electioneering...

An Apology
Peter David Goodwin

In my defense
let me say that I was in a hurry
I was impatient
I'm always impatient at the check-out line
In my defense
let me say that I did not know
that she was a Black woman
how often do you see a Black woman
in a hardware store
In my defense
let me say she looked
as if she was just standing around
chatting, cluttering up the line
In my defense
Let me say she was wearing a tailored tunic,
the same color worn by the store employees
I noticed the attractive tailored tunic
with hints of Scotland and Jamaica
but not her face
and I ignored her
and went straight to the other woman

who happened to be white
and asked her to run up my few purchases
I'm busy, she said
I'm serving this customer, she said
who is ahead of you,
Oh, I said
my apologies, I said—
I didn't—

And now I am the one who is embarrassed
as I stand behind the straight back of a Black
woman wearing an attractive tailored tunic
who probably thinks I am just another racist

I wanted to talk to her
and tell her that I was not a racist
but she never turned her face towards me
and just walked out of the store
not allowing me my apology

The Stone Throwers
Peter David Goodwin

What triggered the memory?
Walking down Fifth Avenue?
The elegant ladies with their shopping bags?
The tourists walking too slowly?
The hustlers peddlers harassing selling trinkets or dollars?
Foreigners definitely. Refugees? Middle Eastern?
Suddenly, I'm back in Tehran—
lost in a strange city
asking a woman for directions, or news,
there were rumors of war around Israel.

Most women in Iran live lives as proscribed
as the cloaks that engulfed them
but this woman wasn't——
this breath-takingly beautiful woman
this blatantly beautiful woman
this flamboyantly beautiful woman
in a bright blue dress
clinging to her body
bold lips, shaded bright eyes
the soft, cream contours of her breasts

not hidden but recalled all these years later.
A shimmering goddess, on her way somewhere,
in a hurry; our conversation was brief.

As she swept on her way, I remarked to my companion,
if she ventured into the market
she would be stoned
(we had met some girls
who had been stoned
for wearing shorts)

Where is she now?
(She? Or her daughters?)
Shrouded in a chador?
Forbidden to show off her figure, her good looks
forbidden to have the pleasure of men looking at her
forbidden to have the pleasure of looking at men
forbidden the pleasure of a little excitement
forbidden the pleasure of taking up space
yet we preferred those places
where a self confident women would get stoned
we were in search of the exotic, the exciting, the danger
and loved to wander the back streets, the markets
with their interesting smells, the spices, the rugs,
the exotic jackets and hats, the hand crafted furnishings,
those places shaded from the sun, dark, mysterious,
where women did not venture
and if they did, were hidden in black
taking up as little space as possible
we expecting that soon
all this would be swept away by an expanding
Americana, its suburbs stretching across Long Island,

across Europe, through Asia and on a Los Angeles,
what a dull future we feared
and wanted to experience it all
before it disappeared.

That may happen one day.
Meanwhile in most places (even here)
the world belongs to the stone throwers.

Bullfight - Holly Tappen

Listen
R. J. Keeler

An echo mixed within its own subtext
like a quiet whisper or celestial music.
Silence arises not just alongside sound,

also within. So attend at every moment
to what's going up around you; every
word, spoken or not, has its very season

as it passes into discourse, raw or empty.
Say, *I have nothing else to say to you*!
(Your heartbeat's adequate to this task.)

A hawk's silence as it passes overhead,
the mouse's rustle in grass below. Who
can hear the sun in one ear and sky

in the other? Or, crisscross a lonely heart,
know its return echo? If you want
pages of dead manuscripts to murmur

to you—there's nothing here to be heard.
Shakespeare's breath a red demon in wait.

Rituals
R. J. Keeler

Burdened by high priests, they bind lesser
and greater gods to our sides; whatever they
may promise, will they favor our fate,
or turn a flat back at us?

The wisdom of an old lead elk graces her
herd's reckoned arc. Raptors and
scavengers circle in wait; sniff, gauge
possibilities. What does she remember—of
what use is she? She's had her run. But
soon, she turns half-back, tosses her life's
learnings astern. These pass to daughters,
even to sons, in turn. Abler rivals arise,
overtake; her finish is unwelcome.

The old elk, now long dead, still holds onto
her charmed carapace. We all unfold small,
hushed hands and receive there her soft,
formal glass—molten spice, a promiscuous
chant. That wise elk's ancient elixir floods
across certain vast oceans of nature. Sour

marsh grass arises, rewards small
grasshoppers that still do hearty work—
useful around late blooms in alpine
meadows.

While, up at terrible altitudes, occasionally
at 40° below zero, greylag geese thrum
down their winter migration, dowsing for
their greener path, for their watery ring—
solid earth, engraved yet foreign—for a
levelling of hearts, for a press to open onto
a rarer faith.

Rituals—well-worn, animal-kind handiworks.
Burnished or unburnished, they seal us in
their rosiness. Flip a fair coin, choose which
door to open. Most everyone knows the
small bite of real fear come between their
charms and a life.

Look at the rising green grass of the
Southern Cross, little distorted from the
Paleolithic; so, rooted in that rise, night
upon night, we grasp at fragmentations.

Reckoning
Jacalyn Carley

Winter's tourniquet tightens,
wrings the white out of a cloud,
cuts off the throb of dawn.
Sacrificed is a limb of horizon
to save the torso of sky.

Abandoned at the curb a boxing glove
lies, buried in brown leaves and grit. A relic,
the fist of a saint who tried too hard. A warning,
to my heart. Throw in the towel. A pandemic fact,
the forecast is for more of the same.

Blown Capacitor - D Ferrara

Last in Line
Kari Despain

I lie on my bed these nights and feel the silence like a smog, the quiet so thick I can hear it. It has a whir like the ocean, which I've been to maybe four times in my life. The train passing on 159th (if I lie still enough, I can feel my bed vibrate while it slithers through the south end of town a mile away). Tonight there is lightning, but the kind that doesn't throw thunder far enough to reach here. And it's April, which doesn't even need the cooler or the fan for rhythm. I've been sheltering-in-place for twenty-nine days under my county's COVID-19 order. Four weeks. An entire month.

I'm an introvert, so it doesn't hurt me like it does some people, but I can feel myself slipping into oblivion. Some of this isolation stuff is easy because I've been doing it on purpose for several years. When I moved to the city three years ago, I was going through a divorce that was mentally and emotionally bankrupting. I underestimated how difficult it can be to lose the identity of couplehood in middle-class, conservative America when a nuclear family splits. Although I didn't want to be married, I wanted claim on that identity for its acceptability, its safety, and its viability. I discovered that it was easier to keep others at arm's length. I was friendly but panicked any time I thought I might be invited to attend a dinner party. I pulled away from social interactions, which is something I had never done before. I dealt with others in a surface-level fashion that I grew to prefer. It required so little of me.

I always believed that isolation happened to people against their best efforts—that some people don't have friends just because they don't. Perhaps sometimes that is the case. But perhaps for many, it's an escape, an act of self-preservation when the self has been lost or at least changed in some traumatic sense. In my case, there were people who reached out while I recoiled. All that was required of me was to meet their reach with honesty and openness, and I found it too difficult. I discovered that if people are avoided for long enough, they will stop reaching. Then the work of isolation is over. One can simply exist. Imagine my relief, after years of thinking I should "be," upon realizing that I could merely exist.

Alone with my own vices this past month, there are places I've fallen into, mostly online. At night, I've been viewing YouTube videos of people bleaching their own hair. I'm not sure what about these attracts me. The anticipation of whether they will get it right, although I'm sure they won't, coupled with the irony of unexpected horror in their expressions as their hair gleams a cartoon orange or yellow? Sometimes their hair is so brittle after the bleaching that it breaks off in clumps. Disappointment in the failed pursuit of beauty.

I've also fallen into the conspiracy world—something I'd never admit to people in person. My favorite at the moment is David Paulides' work concerning people who go missing in the wilderness. It's more than just people getting lost, he claims. He offers no theories on these disappearances, only evidence that something strange is occurring. For decades, people have been reported disappearing, seemingly into oblivion, on hikes and camping trips with friends, leaving no evidence as to where they've gone. These claims have awoken folklore that seemed lost to time until recently and which is now being passed across forums and other forms of response in the online world. The intrigue centers around the question: What takes them?

These disappearances happen in isolation for the most part. Experts offer a few tips to keep from getting lost in the wild: carry both a gun (to call for help) and a GPS transponder (to let people know where you are), tell someone when you expect to be back, and, if hiking in a group, don't be at the end of the line. There is a slew of stories involving hikers going missing in a matter of seconds from the end of a line of hikers. With this last tip in mind, I've reflected on how a group, when hiking, would decide who gets to be at the end of the line. Is this like the trolley question? Decide who would be missed the least if they disappeared?

Another online area I've frequented more is social media. It can make a person feel like they are interacting with others, something I am beginning to miss. I've especially noticed a particular person whom I haven't been in contact with for decades, but who requested my friendship about a year ago. Her name, which she has changed online, is Nona. We grew up in the same small town. During elementary, our class consisted of somewhere between thirty and fifty kids. Our graduating class was about 250. It was hard not to know everyone in our school. You'd think it'd be hard to get lost.

Nona was overweight as a child but, even if that hadn't been the case, she would have still been an atypically large child. She stood head and shoulders above the rest of us by mid-elementary with broad shoulders and long feet. She never had hair past her mid-neck, and it was usually permed so it wore even shorter. Her nose was too small for her face, and her teeth were too tiny for her mouth. As you can imagine, most kids weren't very nice to her. We weren't outright mean, but it isn't nice to always choose someone last for kickball, softball, jump-rope, or soccer.

It wasn't just the fact that Nona was large or somewhat unfortunate in her aesthetic that bred intolerance toward her. She lied. A lot. She told lots of little white lies that were nothing more than annoying, and some blatant, ridiculous lies that left other kids bewildered as to how she may think they would believe her. She told silly lies such as a story about her dad being incredibly wealthy and buying her a horse (that eventually turned into a whole herd of wild horses) that she kept on a huge ranch in California, which she would be going to visit in the summer.

Nona told other lies that were confusing to us. Like the time she convinced a girl in another fifth-grade class to let her wear her arm brace during recess. When someone in class asked why she had a brace on after recess, she said she had hurt herself and been ordered by her doctor to wear it. A few minutes later, the owner of the arm brace came knocking on our classroom door, asking for her arm brace back because her arm hurt. The class giggled and elbowed one another. Nona's face flared blotchy pink with embarrassment, and her jaw clenched, gritting her tiny teeth behind tight lips. The story was passed from group to group at the next recess, loudly, and with stifled laughs loud enough for Nona to hear.

I was reminded of her tendency to lie soon after she entered my social media circles about a year ago. She and her husband were apparently job hunting at the time, and a friend of hers suggested a company in the area where they live. Nona replied to this friend that her husband had already worked there once and been "let go" for some reason. When her husband replied in the conversation that he had *not* been let go, but rather quit, and for completely different reasons than she had described, Nona replied with, "That's what I meant, honey. My phone auto-corrected me."

Nona's social media activity has fascinated me since. She and her husband have had some real financial struggles. She's been very open about their mutual lack of employment, losing their home, moving, then moving again, ultimately ending up in a better situation, for which I'm genuinely glad. I am entertained by her updates concerning her cats, who are afraid of the thunder, her cooking ventures (which are usually a boxed dinner, pictured on a plate set on her legs which are always propped up with bare feet), and hand-made projects she completes and shares. Other people I graduated high school with give her positive feedback, which I believe is genuine. I wonder if we all do it more for ourselves as some kind of atonement for our playground antics that must have continued through middle and high school.

I recently asked a friend who isn't part of Nona's social media circle if they remembered Nona. "OH yeah," was their reply. I didn't ask what exactly they remembered, but since this friend and I didn't share many memories until high school, I assumed they must remember her from high school. I wasn't even sure if Nona had graduated with my class. I couldn't remember one single memory of her in my years after elementary.

I dug out my senior yearbook from the garage. It sits in a tote full of other yearbooks and childhood keepsakes. My first baby doll, my high school cheerleading uniform, a book about elves that my great grandmother gave me when I was three. Sure enough, within the rows of senior pictures, there is Nona in her senior smock that all the girls were made to wear, looking thinner than her elementary days, her blonde hair precise, and her smile straight. She was there.

I looked her up in the index. Nona is referenced six times. I am referenced eight. Voted by the school as "Best Personality" in the class of 1998, I wasn't exactly desirable, but fairly likeable. I was cheerful and non-threatening. I remained quiet at all the proper times that make life easy for others. I didn't complain when something was wrong and laughed at all the right moments. I smiled a lot. I pleased on an exhausting level that I believe has continued in some form or another into middle age.

I'm reminded by the yearbook index that Nona was in the band with me. I remember her being a terrible flutist. It was evident that she never practiced, and it upset me at the time. I'm reminded that she was in the drama club. I begin to remember the faces she gathered with, although I can't remember names.

As an adult, Nona has few friends, it seems. She shared a memory on Facebook this morning--the kind that are generated automatically from previous years.. The photo is captioned: *It's official. Ring is on!* She got engaged four years ago. Three people liked the photo. One person commented: I like it.

Other things I've gleaned from Nona's comments and her shared memories over the past year include that since graduating high school, she had a full career as an EMT, left a physically abusive relationship, lost two infant children to death, and has a daughter who looks just like her but doesn't live with her. This woman is a mystery to me, but it seems that she always was a mystery to everyone around her. We never knew what to believe about her. It's possible that not many people do still. How does someone disappear when they are right there with us? How was it decided that Nona got the position at the end of the line? Was it solely her size in elementary? Was it partly her lies?

Nona and I probably had more in common during our growing years than I previously assumed. We were both people pleasers. She told us lies to try and impress, distract, and interest us. She was following nearly the same formula that I was in those years, but she got it one-off. She put salt instead of sugar into the recipe. She wanted our attention so ravenously. She wanted to be just the sort of girl who wasn't forgotten. And so did I. I simply seasoned my interactions differently than she did.

Judging from her online interactions, I am probably less lonely than Nona, even while maintaining social and emotional distance. In fact, I didn't feel even a little lonely until I stayed inside for a month. This three-year period of isolation has been a baptism of silence for me. A chance to hone my attention to voices that I value. But, like most projects of immersion, one can drown if they stay under too long. I can see this in Nona's evolution into adulthood. I feel culpability in her disappearance. I fear my own.

This week I forced myself to book a campsite near some friends who've invited me to join them for a weekend in October. I promised another we will take a day trip together. I have invited a few over for fish tacos. These things terrify me although I know they are low stakes. I'm likely more scared of myself than them—afraid that I will jump into my pleasing habits. But perhaps during this time in my wilderness of solitude, I have developed the tool I needed all along to see that I, and others for that matter, don't disappear into the background: a sense of permission and the ability to tell others, authentically, where I am.

Pas de Deux - Ralph F. Florio

Heartless
Anita S. Pulier

Once regal and commanding,
our weary hearts droop,
sigh, abdicate power,

reduced by a novel virus
to supplicant, compelled
to bow—to nose, mouth,

face, lungs, and to
cower in the presence
of an elusive enemy.

Mired in the brambles
a desperate struggle
for survival a frantic world
has changed allegiance.

Reluctantly, valentines,
love letters, poems,
Cupid and Eros
are pushed aside, as

melancholic hearts sulk
impatiently in the wings,
like aging screen stars

desperate
for a red carpet comeback.

A Walk in the Park
Anita S. Pulier

Suddenly the everyday is not.
Warmth rushes the Earth
sparking growth.

Streams of light wild with promise
splash sunbeams on tiny buds,
tease wildlife out of dark places.

And there we are, winter clothes
like the layers of our youth, peeled away,
arms entwined, balancing each other,

strolling through
the glorious greening,
gasping at our luck.

Blue Ridge Sky - Patricia A. Florio

Glassy
Barry Lee Thompson

She talks about the first time. It was, she says, during her walk by the river, her daily search for solitude. The bottle was standing upright, catching sunlight, on a fence post near the rail bridge. Wooden fence, empty green wine bottle. Unremarkable.

But then, a vibration. High pitched and faint, like a tuning fork. Not from the bottle, not exactly, but of it. A confidential whispering of its glass body.

And then a train overhead exploded into the reverie. She tried to make out the faces of commuters at the passing windows. All she saw was shapes, passing blurs.

Then the bottle was silent. She walked away, thoughtful. Slowed, looked back. A glint, beckoning. Don't go.

She returned. Picked up the bottle. Swung it, forwards and backwards. Replaced it on the post, adjusted to the same position, label facing the river. She would return the following day to see if it had waited. "Tomorrow," she whispered before leaving.

Next day, the bottle was there, still, smiling. She held it, stroked it, swung it forwards, backwards, sensed its want for flight. Yes, it said. She looked around: nobody else. Here goes. She swung deep, released. The bottle arced high and slow, strange how slow, towards its destiny, towards the bridge wall, impacted then shattered, splinters like happy raindrops in sun rays. A goods train rumbled overhead. When it had passed, silence.

That silence. An absence. Glassy air, settling. The most beautiful sound. She says she had to have it again. And again and again. Now she spends her days seeking it.

Afterdark
Barry Lee Thompson

He prefers the nights. This preference has developed over time, gradually, so that nowadays he rarely surfaces into daylight. His vitamin D comes from a jar, mainly, or from occasional sunlit moments in a quiet corner of the back garden when he's sure the neighbours aren't around. They're nice enough, but he doesn't like to talk anymore. He has begun to forget how to converse, and as he forgets more, and more, it becomes increasingly awkward, and so he wants to do it less, and so on.

At night, down beneath the bridge, little in the way of talk occurs. It's more a place of physical interactions, of silent dances, where people move slowly, take their time.

One night he was pushed into a dank corner by two men, and one of the men took items from his pockets while the other restrained him. But there was no need for the restraint. He wasn't resistant, offered no counter to their actions. He wasn't afraid, either, though no one else was around, but he knew he was supposed to be afraid. And though the men took what they wanted, they were uncertain. Things weren't playing out the way they were meant to. One of the men was rattled. Jittery. It was in his eyes.

Others, maybe, after an incident like this, wouldn't have visited the bridge after dark again. Or at least would have hesitated. But he continued without any pause, no second thoughts, and went down there the very next night as if nothing untoward had occurred. He still thinks about it, though, wherever he goes. It's like a stubborn stain. There have been no such incidents since. There's always the possibility, but such things can happen in the daytime as well, and he still prefers the nights.

First Day Of Summer
Barry Lee Thompson

The heat surprised us in the morning, and by late afternoon it was pressing down. The first day of summer I called it, but Roddy said it was a phantom. We closed the curtains and sat around without clothes. My back was slick with sweat, and the backs of my knees. Roddy touched me there, but he made a face and wiped his hand on the couch. His disgust annoyed me. We argued. I grabbed a towel and my phone and went out the back. He stayed inside.

He sent me a message. Hi Martin, it began. My Sunday name. But the message was full of typos and nonsense. He knew that would make me laugh. I wrote one back, reserved but cordial enough, adding a smile. It went on like that for a while, and in that way things were repaired. I stayed outside though. It was easier than talking.

I heard Pino rustling round in his backyard next door, tapping his dodgy thermometer and tutting. He peered over the fence. "Very warm," he said eventually, a cigarette bobbing at his lower lip. "Beautiful," I said. "Yes, beautiful," he said. He stared, scrunching his eyes against the sun and the smoke. "But maybe you're burning," he said. "Here is better," he said, indicating the shady spot right below the fence. I moved. "That's the way," he said, looking down at me. I closed my eyes. I could hear him standing there a long time, and I kept my eyes shut till he'd shuffled off again.

When it got dusky it cooled but not by much. The air became filled with tiny ashy insects. I dozed to the tickle of papery wings at my eyelids and inside my ear. When I woke it was still balmy, the insects were gone. The moon was too large, unreal, like a painting hanging overhead. The air was perfumed with night-scented flowers and tobacco smoke drifting from somewhere. I turned on the tap at the wall and the hose kicked and spat. I aimed the spray on myself, yelped at the cold, drenched myself. Then I turned the hose and watered the mint in the vegetable patch. The back door opened, and Roddy was there like a naked ghost. "What the fuck," he said. "You'll wake the neighbours." He came over, turned off the tap, but I think he was smiling. "Come inside now," he said, taking the hose from my hand and placing it on the ground. "I'm wet," I said. "It's late," he said. "Come inside."

Struggle
Robert Armstrong

It's a constant struggle,
Fighting this disease,
Living in the ever-present
Shadow of a bottle,
Shaking,
What is normal?
What does it feel like?

Wrestling with my mind
Every day,
No matter how much time
I have under my belt,
How strong I feel,
The bottle looms,
Whispering to me,

In dark corners,
In the light,
Standing in lines at the
Grocery store,

Hitting me out of nowhere,
It whispers in an
Insidious voice,
Clawing at my dreams,
My aspirations,

Staying strong is a struggle,
Talking,
Telling on my demons,
Exposing them,
Exposing myself,

Slaying them with swords
Made of words,
Basking in the sunlight,
In the struggle,
Of life.

Sadness Grown
Robert Armstrong

The blues we cry are born
From broken tears,
Alcohol fueled my madness,
For so many years,

Music so beautiful,
Haunting,
Dreams creating a fog
Blanketing this valley
Of my birth,

Clinging to my heart,
Breaking against the
Shores of the Hudson,
I love to stare and stare,

Washing away the pain as
Another piece,
Fractures from my heart,
Falling into my hands,

Dripping,
Slipping through my
Fingers,

Lazily drifting to
Fertile valley soil,
These seeds of sorrow
Are reborn,
Into an effigy of my
Heart,

An already dying tree,
Born of sadness,
Inside this lonely
Valley,
Of
My
Birth.

Unseen
Robert Armstrong

Sunlight reflects,
Until moonlight
Encroaches,
On the
Impossibilities
Of
Thought,
Patterns lost
In dreams,
Screams playing notes
On a scale,
Only the insane
Understand,
Staring at
Walls,
Moving to
The beat of
Unheard cords,
Bleeding ears from
Scratches,

Never felt,
Unfocused from
What's
Real,
What is,
What can be,
What Isn't.

May 2020
Lara Frankena

At seven it is all birdsong
and bees abuzz in the rosemary,
sky unmarked by either clouds or contrails.
I eke out this early-morning peace
by attending to each plant
with my daughter's painted watering can,
trudging back and forth to the tap
instead of simply unfurling the hose.
On our daily walks I smell my neighbors' roses,
bend heavy lilacs within children's reach.
I argue with my parents over FaceTime.
For want of two apples, a few bananas,
maybe some raspberries
they will leave the house
and endanger their lives?
Here in London, the familiar rattle
of a delivery van sets us salivating.
What might its climate-controlled chambers divulge?
I reread the strawberry and cream lolly box:
At only 111 calories and gluten free

this will transform you
to the beautiful English summer...
If only it read transport, I muse,
and seaside rather than summer.

Chance
D. Chase-Herber

The tailpipe rattles on my Mazda as I throw it into park. Mom's Buick still sits in her parking space, and I feel a punch in the gut when I see the light isn't even on behind the sheers. I lied to Craig, said she was on her way in for the day shift, and she isn't even up.

I sit, torn between anger and fear. Lee probably stopped by last night; I could hear his sleazy laugh through the window when I rolled out of bed and back into my clothes. Why Mom would spend time with a literal slimeball is beyond me...

Except it isn't.

Am I going to walk in to her nodding out in the chair? Will the needle still be sticking out of her arm, the twenty-eight days of rehab and two months of struggle all down the drain?

I take a deep breath, shove hard against the car door. Waiting won't make it better.

"Hey there, little guy. I ain't gonna hurt ya."

My eyes swim with tears, the relief is so strong. "What are you doing, Mom? You're late for work!" I say this to the ass sticking up in the air by the bushes beside the building, all bones since she got in deep with the oxycontin.

"Nikki?" She calls to me through her armpit, something in her hands. "That you?"

No, it's your OTHER only child, but I bite back the sarcasm that only shows up when I shouldn't use it. "Yeah—it's 7:30, Mom. You were supposed to be there a half hour ago. Craig's having a fit!"

She wiggles backwards on her knees and elbows, the something held off the ground.

"Damnit—lost track of the time." She stands up and shoves some mangled bread under my nose. "Here, take it."

I recoil from the wet mess. "What for?"

Her eyes are too bright, the ruin of her teeth between her lips all gray and brown. I never see her outside of work, what with the twelve-hour shifts and the endless overtime. She doesn't bother with lip gloss any more since we all wear masks now, and the gaunt lower half of her face looks more and more like a stranger as time goes on. "This little guy won't come out—he's back there, just shaking. "

She gestures to the bushes with the bread, and I see a quivering lump of brown and white pressed against the cinder block retaining wall.

"You know we can't have dogs here, Mom." I don't tell her there's nowhere farther down to go than the Piney Inn Motel, because it just rubs in the fact that we're already so close to the bottom.

Her face changes, gets red under the winter pale. "You're just like your father was! Always telling me we can't have no dogs! I ain't stupid—I ain't gonna keep him or nothin'. I just wanna get him outta the rain and take him to the shelter."

A big fist squeezes my chest and my eyes burn. I hate myself for looking down at the mildew on the sidewalk, for the way

122

my cheeks flush, for my hand reaching out and taking the bread she's waving around.

"You'll give him the food?"

I nod.

"I just don't want you to lose your job, Ma. There ain't much else around here that pays..."

Her face twitches, a big one that's the whole left side pulling back. "I can talk to Craig."

The words slur through the tense muscles, then she relaxes. "I ain't been late this month, yet."

I don't mention that it's only February 5th. The cold damp shuffles along in a lazy breeze that blows right through my Walmart coat. "Okay, Mom. Just get there safe."

I watch her clamber into the big old car, turn the key a few times, listen to the heavy chug before the motor catches. The tires squeal a little as she pulls out onto the main road, but that's just Mom driving.

Brown eyes watch me from under the bushes, so I watch them back. "I'll just leave this here." He shakes from the cold or the fear, his whole head following my progress to the edge of his hiding place.

I put the bread on the soggy mulch, and I figure that's about that. I stop at the motel door and look back. The pile of mush stands lonely, the sad, liquid eyes on me instead of the food.

Mom would take him into the room and clean him up, give him a bath, make sure he had enough to eat and a bowl of water. Sure, she'd forget all about him when she was high, but in those bouts of sobriety, she'd let him curl up in her lap and feed him so full of treats he'd throw up. I'd probably come home to a warm spot on the bed and a pillow full of drool, and she'd put on the pouty face that hadn't aged well every time I brought up how he needed to go to the pound.

I turn my back and open the door with judgment on my shoulders. I might have done exactly what Mom told me, but I hadn't done what she meant.

"Stop half-assing everything."

Dad might have said those words to me at least twice a day from my first bad report card in the third grade to the day the cancer killed him, but today, it is my voice saying them. Their big teeth rip open something I didn't think could hurt any more.

The dog limps towards me, his tail wagging back and forth a few times. He's beagle-shaped, stocky gone a little skinny, but not starving. His right front paw doesn't work too good, but he gives me the kind of grin Daddy had when he'd drunk just enough to be nice and the hope lights up his eyes the same way thinking about leaving this godforsaken town lights up mine.

I know I shouldn't, but I hunker down in a chorus of popping joints still stiff from twelve hours standing on a concrete floor and shoving one box into another. "How'd you end up here, buddy?"

The tail wags a little harder, and he licks the hand I stretch out. I pat his head, the white hairs mixed in with the brown just like the pony I rode that one time at the fair when we had money, and when his tail goes, his hips follow along in a gentle wiggle.

He smells like coconut Suave shampoo after his bath. He licks the water coming out of the faucet and I laugh, and I don't immediately realize it's me because it actually sounds happy.

We eat dinner in the kitchenette—me, the turkey platter, him, the Salisbury steak Mom and I can't stomach.

He nibbles the steak delicately, then laps up all of the gravy and the mashed potatoes. He skips the corn.

"Good choice." I nod, and his tail goes. "That corn will make your intestines explode."

We watch *The Princess Bride* on cable. His eyes and his gray muzzle poke out of a cocoon of towels. He likes Westley and Buttercup, but hides his face when Prince Humperdink is onscreen. He's small and neat on Mom's side of the bed, the sunlight slicing through the curtains that don't close all the way, making his towel cave golden, magical

Gray muzzles don't get you adopted..

He limps to the front door when I come out of the bathroom and waits, eyes on the handle. I turn it and marvel that he has not barked a single time, watch as he piddles at the edge of the garden. I think to grab one of the yellow Dollar General bags floating around the room, but he doesn't poo and I am grateful—I would have to take it to the Dumpster, or live with the smell.

He curls up into a cat-like ball, his back against Mom's pillow, his nose close to my face.

"Danny. What do you think of Danny?"

He opens his eyes the littlest bit.

Danny licks my nose, then settles with a sigh of Salisbury steak breath, coconut fur, and a little touch of old dog.

Danny was a boy I knew in high school. He was always nice to me...not the creepy kind of nice like just trying to get into your pants. The real kind of nice, like would actually want to dance at the prom.

He worked nights at the convenience store. One night was really bad. They shoehorned his picture into the In Memoriam spread in my sophomore yearbook at the last minute, and everyone said how they knew Rick was a bad kid before he dropped out and started robbing people. It was only a matter of time, they said.

And everyone just waited for that time to come.

"We'll get you a collar tomorrow." There's a bare spot on Danny's neck, where a collar wore his fur down to the skin. Even the muscles are molded into a groove, the memory of the people who used to love him.

Danny sighs in his sleep, somewhere in doggy dreamland. Seems like a pretty good place to be. I'm thinking the first step to getting there is closing your eyes...so I close my eyes.

And it's a damn good place to be.

Julie's Garden During the Pandemic
Julene Waffle

You tell me before our workshop that your catbird
has gone away, taken his stolen songs with him south.
Your chipmunk has tucked his last black oil sunflower seed
into the heart of some naked tree. The snow
has covered fall's final flower; only the stalks of a few
forgotten seed rounds needle themselves through new snow.

I think of last spring:
your crocus greens fanning out in circles that I didn't see,
the daffodils and snowbells waking early to sew the spring
into the quilt of your backyard,
your Jacob's ladder, the tulips kissing the patchwork sky,
then summer's peonies and daylilies
by fireworks and Fourth of July. Daisies by August
danced with bee balm amid hot pink handfuls of phlox.
Thistle and sunflowers were the last to dip their reverent heads
to the majesty of passing fall.

Your hands nurtured them all,
the same hands that would have set the patio table

with a vase dressed in a few of your favorites,
the same hands that would have poured sun tea
over ice cubes from your freezer,
the same hands that would have danced their way
through our lazy conversation last summer,
except that we never had the chance.

As your rose-breasted grosbeaks and cardinals,
your chickadees and your bully blue jays
color the branches of your silver maple today,
and as your chipmunk burrows into his torpor,
know that even though I never set foot in your garden
as planned, I was there with the hope of it,
and none of this, not even you or me of this very moment,
this poem, or our friendship, would have ever happened at all
if it had not been for that very same thing that kept us apart.

A Pandemic Irony
Julene Waffle

Sea turtles spend most of their lives alone
swimming oceans, searching for food. They live
50 years in solitary submersion.
Alone, by choice, they see the world through waves.

What was not natural
was being 96, swimming in loneliness,
waving to grown children
through nursing home windows, living in fear.

Children staring at computer screens
learning to navigate the ocean of their futures
without sails, without rudders,
without hands on oars.

Governors closing businesses,
farmers dumping tanks of milk in gutters,
people losing jobs, being labeled non-essential.
Over three million lives lost.

But the sun still rose and set;
the tides still rolled. The earth
still wound her way around the sun. Crops
still embraced the sky while our lives

crawled cautiously to stand still.
No soccer games. No drama club. No choir.
No travel. No birthday parties. No sleepovers.
No eating out. Those seemed small prices to pay.

And so loneliness dragged from summer
into long and empty winter.
But in that space—in that expanse—
there was something: There was time—

Time to focus on children, play board games, play outside.
Time to talk to trees and listen for their responses.
Time for phone calls, Zoom calls, calls to write letters.
Time to craft, to bird watch, to ride bikes,

to read for pleasure, to take long baths.
Time to declutter and find lost things.
Time to self-educate, self-evaluate.
Time to exercise. Time to think.

And now what was normal before
looks something like that normal again.
Baseball games are scheduled.
Brides confirm wedding guests.

Children are sitting in classrooms.
Fitness centers and diners have reopened,

Vaccines are invisible shields.
And we are happy

for the return to something familiar,
for feeling safer. But
I can't help the undercurrent
running under the loss and waste of it all.

No matter how much I want to return to familiar shores,
a part of me longs for the quiet and time just to be.

Me and My Shadow - Patricia A. Florio

The Year Of Cortisol
Gale Martin

You heard it was the Year of the Rat—a yang year, yang being the active male principle of the universe and the complement to yin.

You know 2020 was also the Year of the Nurse, according to the World Health Organization, because it's the year your daughter started her nursing career two weeks after the pandemic knee-capped the United States of America, the irony of which will haunt you until she is vaccinated in 2021.

Looking back over the past twelve months, you would like to offer the universe another organizing precept. You have irrefutable proof it was the Year of Cortisol.

You know cortisol is your body's natural alarm system. You learned somewhere that it's your predominant stress hormone. Whenever you're thrown into fight-or-flight mode, cortisol kicks in. Maybe you first received that information in tenth-grade health class.

"Cortisol is a go-juice that revs up your senses and helps you cope in the face of danger, emergencies, and threats. Your ancestors needed this stuff when they lived in caves and were chased by saber-tooth [sic] tigers. It was kill or be killed," sweet, smiley Mr. Graef had said during the fall of 1973 because the second half of the year he always taught Driver's Ed.

You ponder whether saber-toothed cats lived during the same time as early man since Mr. Graef was no anthropologist. You never thought about "Smiley" Graef or his health class or that gigantic incisor jutting up from his lower front teeth until 2020, like a saber-toothed Homo sapiens.

Okay, maybe once before you thought of him when one of your incisors began crowding out your own lower teeth at the same time you career-changed to become a classroom teacher in your forties, circa 2001. You didn't want to be called "Old Snaggletooth" behind your back while parading in front of a room full of eighth-graders, all eyes staring, wondering why you obtained a master's degree to teach the eight parts of speech but never invested in your smile. So, you did—the only 40-something with braces you knew.

Smiley (that's what you kids called him) had warned that the body is not supposed to have elevated levels of cortisol raging through it permanently. That was the main reason you convinced your mom it was okay to divorce your dad eons ago, once you had your driver's license, because your dad used to drive you to a lot of places, too.

"Mom," you had said. "He threatens at least one of us every day. He hits you, and he will do it again. Please, listen to me. If you don't leave him, all the stress he creates all the time will hurt you," remembering how two years later, your mother had a stroke at age 50, permanently stealing her mental and physical faculties and almost killing her.

Akin to the chickenpox virus lying in wait so it can resurrect itself as shingles disfiguring your entire face and neck until any living family members confused you for the Elephant Man.

Smiley's warning lay dormant for the next two decades. Until the Year of the Rat. The year that proved a megalomaniacal racist mafia boss with the ethics of an alley cat crossbred with a murderous pig was punching far above his weight when it came to handling his big-boy job and oh, yeah, the pandemic, too. Also in dealing with a modicum of competence with the world's biggest economy tanking in March. Not to mention the protests against systemic racism in the US justice system overtaking the country. You would be remiss if you didn't mention the ceaseless lies spewed and perpetuated by Trump on every platform—"the election was rigged," "Sleepy Joe Biden has dementia" and "I won this election by a landslide"—that you couldn't retreat from or perhaps didn't try hard enough to, so, in your desperation, you kept yourself apprised of the latest calamity by tuning in.

You needed to document via self-observation and scrutiny whether consistently elevated cortisol levels exacerbated anxiety, depression, concentration and memory problems, weight gain, and heart disease, or whether old Mr. Graef was perpetuating #FakeNews nearly 50 years before the term was injected into popular vernacular like hydroxychloroquine because those many years ago, you and the rest of America trusted Walter Cronkite, considering him the exemplar among many ethical journalists.

You remember feeling helpless when the governor put your state on lockdown. How could an entire commonwealth that is 300 miles wide, east to west, be locked down in the first place? Whenever you're standing at the kitchen sink these days, you spy a fat plastic tub overflowing with dozens of wine corks because, during the lockdown, that self-same governor closed state-run liquor stores (non-essential businesses, he deemed them). Following the cratering of your 403B and losing 15 years of investments, slim bottles, fat liters, and entire boxes of wine (on sale for $21.99 in grocery stores) were essential to wholly numbing that goddamn fight-or-flight instinct overtaking every waking hour.

During the early months of the pandemic, you were all about flight—mentally removing yourself from your life as you had lived it—because day-to-day life was stimulating your cortisol to elevated levels never sustained before. You ate CBD gummies and soaked in CBD bath bombs. You did Vinyasa yoga. You attempted cooking therapy, preparing gourmet foods and complex recipes, many of which celebrated (you whisper) saturated fats.

You noticed newfound belly fat flopping over your work sweatpants either from the increased wine intake or stepped-up cortisol or both, and started walking the rescue dog four to five times a day briskly, timing yourself, getting that heart rate elevated 15 minutes a pop.

Then you watched an officer kneel on George Floyd's neck for eight minutes. You could no longer focus. You stopped reading. Anything that brought pleasure. You didn't deserve pleasure. Instead, you watched Channel 6, cringing as a mob torched West Philadelphia blocks from where your daughter lived, the self-same daughter easing people's suffering serving a Center City hospital in Philly, a coronavirus hotspot, who hardly deserved to have her third-floor walk-up go up in flames. But then you considered that a lot of people of color were murdered for the crime of being Black.

You decided to fight. You consumed news every day, sent contributions to politicians willing to stand up to the Grifter-in-Chief, shared your woke news on your social media platforms, scaring away followers and lifelong friends.

Even though you switched from fight mode back to flight mode, cortisol could not have cared less. It instinctively coursed through your veins con gusto.

During a routine October checkup, your nurse practitioner railed at you for your high blood pressure. "What are you doing?

It's 146/84. You should be taking your blood pressure every day. Get that cuff. Change your diet."

You purchased a blood pressure cuff on Amazon, deciding it was time to resume fighting. You cut out fruit juices, cut down on coffee and salt, ate more fruits and vegetables, and kept power-walking the dog, perhaps more than the dog herself wanted to be walked. 120/78.5

Even though it was the Year of the Rat, Trump lost. While you know that the self-same Rat of the Chinese zodiac is totally unlike Trump because people born in the Rat year tend to be optimistic and energetic, likable by all, you still can't divorce yourself from the Western view of rats. Filthy, disease-laden, deadly vermin.

Like a rat fleeing a sinking ship, Trump fled to one of his premier golf courses after he lost reelection. You have to wonder whether the Year of the Rat was more apt a metaphor for 2020 than Chinese mythology intended.

Since last April, coronavirus advanced, wildfires scorched, the economy hemorrhaged, toilet paper vanished, hornets murdered, concentration evaporated, unemployment soared, savings accounts vaporized, Black people bled, protests raged, Minneapolis and Portland and Philadelphia burned, bad cholesterol escalated, RGB died, coronavirus surged, Trumpists lied, holidays fizzled, legislators contrived, Trump incited, Capitol ransacked, blood pressure escalated, insurrection foiled, Antifa blamed, Trump impeached, excess pounds lost, yin rose, Texas froze, Ted rationalized, stimuli spent, vaccinations increased, blood pressure stabilized, vaccinations stalled ...hospitalizations climbed.

Through it all—the unrelenting reporting of all the bad, the ugly, the unfathomable, the horrific, the obscene, the unconscionable—on every network, cable station, news outlet, and social media channel, it's fight. Flight. Fight. Flight.

It's cortisol in a landslide.

What I Know
Rachel Evans

It's hard to finish the cookies you left.
Maybe because you didn't really leave
them. You left us,
and the cookies remained.

Of course, it's not your fault.
You couldn't have known that
one Sunday night, just two
days before Donald Trump would
officially be our ex (not our president),
you would step out of the shower,
admire the sunset over the Hudson
from your bedroom window
   one final time
and go to sleep,
never to wake again.

You couldn't have known that movers
would pack everything in your small apartment.
And I mean Every Little Thing,

from the salt and pepper packets you get with takeout
to your underwear
and your jewelry
and your mah-jong tiles
and your unopened glasses
all your little things and your big things
all you owned on this earth
haphazardly boxed up
and dropped at my doorstep.

How can anyone ever really know anything?

I'm not sure what you would say
about your box of Tate's Cookies
getting stale on top of my refrigerator.
Or your last bag of M&Ms sitting unfinished in my pantry.
So few remain: four red, two yellow, three green and a
solitary blue
gathering and melting at the bottom
of the plastic (not my hand).
I think you'd probably ask what I was waiting for.
I don't know, I would say. You, perhaps.

Tonight, I dare say it,
I let myself taste the sweetness of your favorite cookies
once again.
My lips wrapping around the cookie dust,
my teeth biting down,
each crunch its own funereal hymn.
Each swallow made you smile in my mind.

I only ate one.

It was all I could muster the courage for.
But as I stood in the kitchen chewing
I heard your high-pitched child's giggle
laughing at me
like I had snuck it while you weren't looking.
And suddenly you were there
alive, breathing, congregating, pulsing
in the room with me
as I finished the cookie.

There is just so much we can't know,
from moment to moment
from inhale to exhale
from life to death.
But this I can promise you, this I know:
I will be back for more.

Grief Interrupted - D Ferrara

COVID Quiet, 2020
Diane Valeri

The world stood still,
but it was not quiet.

We hid from workplaces
to remote places,
meeting rooms
now virtual rooms.

I wrote my will.

Digital schools education
transformed.
Smartphones became essential workers
for the coveted vaccines.

Frozen in place,
melting,
Twitter bubbled into a take-over.
Inequality simmer into murder.

The world stood still,
but it was not quiet.

Woman With Square - Holly Tappen

Aftermath
Helen McDonald

South wind skims
valley floor
a mountain wave
to flood-bathe searing skin

Parched gums let loose
their dust coats
shake out seeds
and galls and tiny ants

sucked up
in the whipping
cooled now and buffeted

I brace hard
do not lose ground
My feet take root

I hold on
hold on

and watch
the dying embers
of my ruined life

COVID Lockout (haibun)
Helen McDonald

I cannot see my mother. Nor my mother-in-law. The women whose presence in this world render me still the child, are shut away. Cut off. For years I have cared for these matriarchs. Ever the child, though I have children of my own, a grandchild. Now I can't. Not yet.
Maybe never.

pruning in the
early morning
old roses

Restoration
Helen McDonald

I wish I had a broom and could climb
mini-sized into your beautiful brain
to scrub and clean punctured vessels
and take a tiny needle and thread
sew up the holes and make it perfect again

Your beautiful brain
shuddering, in spasms
darting down down extremities
to shut them down, sever sensation
let slip the beauty of a full curved lip

Give me needle and thread
and I will repair
remake you with your sharp clear thoughts
magician
solver of problems

The gods are jealous
but we don't let them near
we adapt, deflect, adapt again
Whatever they hurl we dodge and weave
and nothing rocks us

Make me tiny
my fingers swift
Let me repair you
and defeat the gods
Again

Photograph - David R. Brubaker

Twice Born
Babitha Marina Justin

A kind nurse comes
with a cathartic enema kit
before each surgery,
I feel like Gandhi.

Life blurs between
the walls and
the operation table
spluttered with blood and
too many births.

between my breath
and the mask, anesthesia
takes off its opium wings.
I like this onerous feeling.
The anesthetist asks
if my firstborn is a boy,

I am even impressed by
his remarks on the persistence
of the crimson lipstick

that the nurse wipes off my mouth
with deft disdain.
I may fall in love with him
during the limen,

I begin to count,
first my blessings and then
numbers, at times, inverted them,
my parched lips recite litanies
those years of rebellion
have not forgotten.
With a fervent Lord's prayer,
I wait for the mask to descend
and my masks fall, one by one.

As the lights dim,
I'm eased in my hypnosis,
I fly like an angel
to witness myself
laid out like lard on the operation table.
I'm a featherweight Ariel
gazing down at the scissor-happy surgeon,
her bevvy of nurses, the kind anesthetist
and my own morphined Caliban.

I fly,
I sink,
I come to.
Spasms of slow,
searing,
serrated pain:
I am alive
          once again.

Toilet Paper Panic
Joel Savishinsky

Plagues produce delusions as well as disease and death. COVID-19 has, sadly, been no exception. In the fateful early months of 2020, myths and misinformation were quickly spawned, as if the germ theory of infection had become obsolete and a medieval faith in spontaneous generation had been re-born in the medium of social media. The deformations of thinking about how to cope with the virus and its consequences were as much political and behavioral as medical. People quickly came to fear shortages of critical supplies as much as, if not more than, they worried about getting sick. And among the most targeted of their concerns was running out of the wherewithal for personal hygiene and indoor sanitation, especially disinfectants and what the advertising geniuses had cleverly and euphemistically re-labeled "bathroom tissue."

The run on the supermarket shelves was on.

Recent psychoanalytic explanations for America's toilet paper panic offer a helpful Freudian perspective. However, there is also a cultural dimension that has not been fully considered. When Americans travel abroad, visiting developing or third world countries with challenging arrangements for relieving and then cleaning oneself, they invariably come home and love to tell tales -- not about the cultural, historical or natural wonders they have seen—but rather about their adventures and misadventures trying to poop and pee. Why the narrative fixation in our society on stories of excretion?

Among the features of American culture we love to brag about are the qualities of our "Holy of Holies,[1]" the bathroom. The technical ingenuity, the immaculate conception of the entire arrangement, and the aesthetic splendor of the experience are, we believe, the envy of the world. Americans love to accompany their bragging with boasts of derring-do about where and how they have made doo-doo. Thus, the anal fixation is more than just Freudian, and transcends early developmental challenges of retention and release, control and continence. We have turned it into a rectal celebration of our homes and our valor. The fear of inadequate toilet paper threatens to undermine the cultural hegemony that both sets us apart and has long licensed us to dump on the rest of the world. Perhaps, as we try to learn the lessons of our latest disorder and our disordered lives, the time has finally come for Americans to find a better way to clean up their act and take a closer look at themselves in the bathroom mirror.

---

[1] Horace Miner: "Body Ritual Among the Nacirema," American Anthropologist 58 (3): 503-507 (1956).

Witches' Solstice–A History
Mary Kay Rummel

December 2020

What do they say about
the ceremonies of our bodies,
our innocence of flesh?

In our scry we see the cities in ruin
toads with pulsing throats on the walkways.
Walled gardens surrounded by sand
lions guarding the gate.

We exist in the music of the present
above the setting canoe moon
wreathed in sunset pink.

Worshipping Jupiter and Saturn—lovers
moving slowly toward each other,
for eight hundred years,
we call into our world
the power of conjunction.

In the dark wood we praise the meadow
sunlight on blue hills
the valley that used to be home
where the bear eats night's fallen apples
then rolls down the road to sleep.

Near the holy well a grey sign: says
If your prayer is for the dead
Walk over the stream,
If for the living
Walk through the water.

The apples are dry, the she bear sleeps.
The stream bed awaits our feet,
sings our new and ancient ways.

The Deep End
Mila Lachica

Summer sun is burning
and yet we reach out for more
and for each other,

as slowly we drown
in six feet of air between us.
Our deep end, we think

or the world's, as we mask
half in fear and confusion,
our best effort to smile unseen.

Our laughter smothered,
voices unclear, but still loud
with words that own us.

Our grief we breathe in
as we breathe out hope
in little bubbly spurts,

bravely owning our words:
surely, this deep end
must lead to the shallows.

A Reader's Plague
Mila Lachica

A little hardbound copy, dust jacket creased, edges torn,
paper yellowing but still soft, over half a century old.
A dollar, yells the flea market vendor, letting go
of the day's treasure, *The Plague* by Albert Camus.

It gets a new home, shelved for a year or so, stuck
between Vonnegut's *Cat's Cradle* and Dante's *Inferno*
until one spring day, a self-crowned virus is named,
bringing the world down to its knees; and all is quiet,
and time is found aplenty, and this time for Camus.

The flipping of the page is slow as words meander
in the ridges of the brain, through a town like any other,
its people strange, no stranger than that of the next.
Then rats are coming out in hordes, mouths gasping for air,
teetering, dying before perplexed, horrified humans.

But the next flip of the page is halted as a fruit fly hovers,
settling on a tray of overripe bananas. Muffins,
screams the reader's baker brain.

TURMOIL AND RECOVERY

Soon, fingers knock at Google's recipe door
for a whole wheat, maple-sweetened banana muffin,
with some oats, crushed nuts and sprinkles
of sugar and cinnamon.

And Camus has to wait,
yet again.

Carmen is Missing
Lori M. Myers

I remember those dark brown eyes, big and round, filled with fear. She was new to this country, she'd told me in a whisper, surveilling the store as if someone were about to pounce on her from behind, her head darting back and forth like a scared puppet. I told her that her secret was safe with me; there was no reason to be paranoid. She cocked her head slightly, revealing the sparkle of the gem studs in her ears, the fine hairs nesting at her neck, the chiseled chin.

"What is this? Poranoi?"

"It's when you think someone or something is after you, but there really isn't," I answered. "It's all in your head."

She stared at me, her eyes narrowing enough that the whites disappeared. "Is not in my head. Is real."

At that moment I fell in love with her. Then she told me her first name: Carmen.

I told her I'd wait outside until lunchtime and we'd go to the diner across the street. She agreed, and I stood on the sidewalk watching her through the window as she replenished the avocados, tomatoes, and heads of lettuce in the produce section. The glass reflected images behind me of mothers dragging kids, old men shuffling in and out of the store, and nerdy high school boys with acne-filled faces scurrying around the parking lot and gathering stray carts. The idea that any of these people would be after Carmen for any reason made me laugh, and I told Carmen that as we sat across from one another in a red plastic booth downing hamburgers dripping with ketchup and sipping sodas. I slurped the last drops in the glass and noticed some heads turn toward me.

"Not nice." And then she looked down. She didn't want any sort of attention directed toward us. The more invisible she was, the safer she felt.

In her broken English, she told me how she'd crossed the border with her mother and little brother, swimming across the river, crawling through thick brush and thorns, fearful of being captured and returned back to Mexico where violent cartels ruled neighborhoods. One hot afternoon, she said, she heard the border patrol on the other side of the sycamores where they rested. Her brother screamed as the men descended, and as if by instinct, their mother leapt to protect him. Carmen crawled away on her belly and hid behind several Esperanza shrubs, her yellow-colored dress blending in with the yellow flowers.

"I hear their screams," she said, her mind now hundreds of miles away. "I run and run."

"Where is your mother and brother?

"Yo no se. They gone. I cannot look for them because they will find me."

Pain formed on her face, guilt for sure, and the constant worry and wondering about their fate. In an instant, she had chosen freedom and safety, but in her soul, she knew that her mother and brother were not given those options. I wanted to try and understand her circumstances, to feel all that she was feeling, and I could tell that she noticed my efforts.

162

"You not know what this is like, what I went through. Don't try."

I told her how I'd been bullied as a kid, how I had to look over my shoulder from grade school to high school, and that noticing kids grouped together made my hands tremble and the blood drain from my face. The idea that someone might grab my shoulder, turn me around, and punch me so hard while others laughed and encourage the offender to continue the assault was a comparable fear. Wasn't it?

"Not the same," she said. "You are safe somewhere, someplace. You lock the door. Watch television. Eat chips. No one bothers you. I can lock door, too. But if someone knocks on door, it's over."

No one asked questions at the grocery store, she said. Sure there were suspicions, but the management needed low-wage workers, so they kept everything under wraps. The local church also stayed mum about the undocumented individuals and families who showed up on their doorstep. They did as much as they could to help find places for them to live or other families with whom they could stay temporarily until they got on their feet. Carmen got lucky in that the store manager, who had come to the United States due to similar turmoil in his birth country of Colombia, took a particular liking to her. I wondered how deep this "liking" was and what she may have given him in return.

"Mi amor?" She clasped her hands over to mouth to stifle a laugh. "No, no! He un hombre viejo. Old. Old man."

Relief washed over me as did my fascination with her, yet there were no signs of reciprocation. At least none that I could determine.

She murmured gracias when I paid the bill and as we left, I offered to walk her home. She refused, said she'd told me too much already, and the next thing I knew I was watching her, her back to me, her hips swinging in some innate rhythm. She turned around one time then waved me away with a hand, signaling me to leave so I wouldn't see which direction she was heading. I mouthed "goodbye" to her. She kept on walking and disappeared into the crowd. She never gave me her address.

Over the next month, I'd memorized her work schedule and feigned getting groceries, even holding a fake shopping list. I'd make believe I was a stranger and ask her where the plums were knowing full well they were right there in front of us. I'd make her laugh at our improvisation as we continued to play the roles of employee and customer. I'd complain about the prices and she'd tell me in broken English to shop somewhere else.

Afterwards, I'd wait at the big window until her shift ended, and we'd have dinner or just walk around town holding hands until the streetlamps and neon signs came on. Then we'd go our separate ways. I think I missed her the most as I walked home alone. The aroma of her, the sparkle of her earring when she'd put her hair behind one ear cloaked me in both comfort and unease. Maybe this was what it was like. Being on the edge and not knowing. Being good and realizing that bad people could do bad things to you. That "escape" is a made-up word without definition. That its existence is a joke. There is no escape. Not in truth.

Our get-togethers went on like this until the pandemic hit. Then everything changed. The grocer where she worked closed its doors with a sign in front that read, "We hope to reopen soon. Stay safe." She had shared her email address with me, a mash of numbers and symbols, but I was to only contact her in an emergency and even then to write cryptically as if my message had been sent to the wrong person. She made me promise this because she feared being traced, being found, hearing the knock at the door.

We were all in lockdown now. This was an emergency. I had to see her, so I set up a Zoom account and copied/pasted step-by-step instructions for her to do the same. I emailed her with a date and time when we could communicate. The meeting date I'd proposed came and went, then another and another. I'd log on and wait for her to appear on screen. I'd have it on for hours and still no Carmen. Days passed without a word. I worried and paced and checked my email every other minute. I just wanted to make sure she didn't forget about me, hear her voice, make sure she was okay. I wasn't about to give up on Zoom meets. I continued doing it and notifying her, but I found myself staring hour after hour at a black empty square.

One day, I was sitting in front of the screen eating pizza when the black box came to life. Wavy lines indicated that it was connecting to audio. My heart beat so loud that I thought it would explode out of my chest. I leaned forward and the pizza dropped to the floor. I sat there frozen, fearing that the slightest movement might make everything crash. I waited as the lines disappeared and a name appeared at the bottom corner: "Al." That was her nickname for her brother, Alphonso. No one would know that except the two of us, one of the few facts she entrusted me with. The box on the screen stayed black for over an hour, then it disappeared. Mania set in, and I scheduled five more Zoom meets overnight and then for the rest of the week.

I waited. Again. Several days later, I was watching the news, my laptop balanced on my thighs. I was drifting in and out of sleep and didn't notice the wavy lines this time or the name "Al" in the black box. It was the music that woke me up, faint yet distinctive, maraca beads pinging against each other in syncopation with a guitar and violin. I listened and stared, my shaking hands pleaded in the chat window for the receiver to turn on their video. I hoped it was Carmen. The music kept playing, the style I recognized as

Mexican but classier than what was performed by those roaming restaurant bands dressed in tacky vests and sombreros.

"Carmen?" I said out loud. "Is that you?"

The box remained dark. Then it told me that whoever was on the other end had left the meeting.

Leaning my head against the seatback, I settled my thoughts on the full moon filtering through the blinds, the silence that once was life before quarantine. I wondered if this was some sort of joke that Carmen was playing on me, like testing me if I had the sort of patience and persistence it took to wait for her to show up, if she ever did show up.

I drifted off again until my email notification dinged. She had been waiting for me to show up on Zoom for more than forty minutes. I rushed to open up the window. Now the box wasn't dark. It had one of those fake computer backgrounds that people put up behind them mainly so others don't see a messy room or to give off the idea they are vacationing at a resort. This background was an outdoor shot filled with all sorts of trees bordered by a wide body of water. The river moved, the trees danced in the wind. There were some yellow flowers in the distance and behind that a wall trailing with vines.

As I called her name again, the screen went dark and then it was just me alone staring at my own reflection. I wanted to give up, but there was nowhere else to go, nothing else to do. I turned off my laptop and laid down on the couch.

For the next few days, I refused to go online. The frustration I felt was palpable and there were moments of rising rage. It was like the bullying of my youth was happening all over again. I ate and read, conversed long distance with a neighbor, and heard from a friend who chastised me for not answering an email he'd sent two days ago.

"When you've read it, get back to me right away. Okay?" he said.

I logged into my email and there was another notice that Carmen had been waiting in a Zoom meet for as many days as I'd been computer-free. I logged on. The screen wasn't black this time. A photograph popped up; Carmen, smiling at the camera, her arms around an older woman and a young boy, the lines of fear replaced with a smile. Carmen's head rests atop the boy's, and happiness radiates in her eyes, something I'd never seen in the months we'd been together. The few furnishings in the photo are utilitarian; a cot on the floor, clothes hanging on an inside line, a rustic table and chairs, a small bowl of fruit nearby. She wears a bright yellow dress, her one earring sparkles in the sun beaming into the room where they sit.

She writes in chat. "Gracias for your friendship."

I respond with a heart and thumbs-up emoji. It was all I could do.

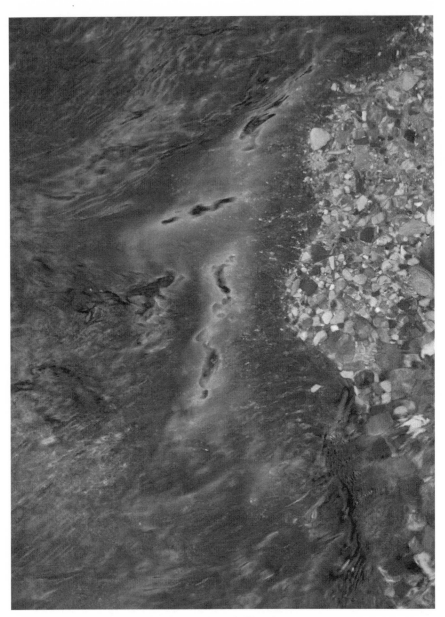

Photograph - Jeff Talarigo

Construction/Deconstruction
Dawn Leas

We worked well together.

He eyed straight lines
with laser-level precision,
did mental math quicker
than blink of an eye.

I kept tidy paperwork piles,
always stacked
books
symmetrically.

We were building a fortress,
one to house our retirement.

Storms approached.

Who doesn't love a good, hard rain?
Flash and sizzle of lightning?
Rolling boom of thunder?

Everyone needs a little ground
shaking now and again.

One morning, we woke to find
we'd read the wrong plans.
Built a wall, not a fortress.

Yes, we worked well together –

until I broke us
apart like a wishbone.

These Days
Dawn Leas

Fear is a heavy coat to wear
day in, day out.

Let the fog hover.
Let the river flow.
Let the in-between of conversations
be still.

Winter never got feet under it, never got full
sails up. Simply drifted away.

Now, a spring born of illness.

Welcome daffodils and dandelions.
   Anything willing to grow.

People will come together.
People will fall apart.

Like the hotel we lived in back in '82
until our new house was ready.

Now empty. Broken windows.
Tossed mattresses
and dressers heaped in the parking lot.

The rain spits today. As if it knows
its chance is only 50-50.

Stop spinning.

Let the wind chimes guide you.

(En)During the Plague
Dave Sims

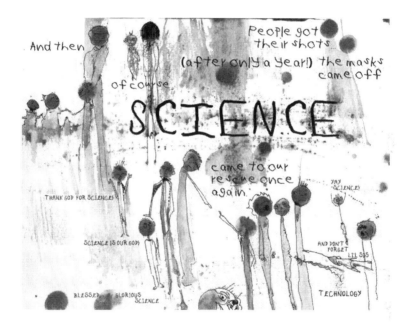

Sure, we all knew there were still VARIANTS lurking out there...but we'd all learned by then to be wary of STRANGERS and don't be expecting any HANDSHAKES or HUGS any time soon...ever...

OF COURSE

trust no one...ever!

the whole world is tainted now...

Cosmic Tilt - Carol MacAllister

The Cat
Bissera Videnova

Reached his hand
to pet her
just
as you caress a street cat
instinctively
then
carefully
washed his hands after that
just in case

bought a frank
for the cat
who
didn't reveal herself.

One or two kitty-kitties
hung
over
in her back,
looked aside.

She wasn't hungry,
she withered from the soap
people used to wash with.

The Last One
Bissera Videnova

The last one in your life
is not that one, which trots about boldly in your dream,
you are speaking something in your language.

It's not that one for which
you fight with dragon and brothers
you offer a sour apple as ripe.

It's not the one that transforms you into a lizard
that bites your tail,
you run away out of your skin.

It's not the one which rips her womb,
you hear your name multiplied.

It's not that one with a bust like oranges,
you drink fresh juice under the tight sweater.

It's not the other one that gets out of the herbarium
you decorate your boutonniere.

It's not a friend who is chasing you
with the hell of a good intention,
you are looking like an old dog.

The one you keep for last
is a Sherpa
with equipped heart
who carries you out the snow of your snowdrifts
on the ridge of the mountain.

Instead of two coins
fallen stars settle
upon your eyelids.

Reasonable People
Bissera Videnova

The reasonable people change the channels
click, click, click—up, down, and back
it's summer
the ones without air-conditioning open the windows
the others carry off the hit easily
72° Fahrenheit in the office, 74° Fahrenheit in the car
at home or at the place where they sleep (home they don't have)
like many degrees, they appraise
according to the understanding of what's useful and harmful
they are surfing. It's summer
on the Facebook pages or are downloading
series—the heavy rope of the social acceptance
they are surfing on the waves of fashion
on the pages of new spa and resorts
everyone in separate rooms with separate air-conditioner
there are no more people who shout and quarrel
in the morning to low eyes
the children are not in a rush to come to the aid of the neighbors
upstairs with groaning and moaning. It's summer
they are surfing through the vampire games
on the locked-with-passwords channels
and they know that the passwords are easy to guess
four zeros or one to four

The reasonable people struck down by the hit
change the channels
click it's not heard, but I get startled
the steady interval of different lights
shines on your sweaty body
I expect it to move on
to a place on which to sleep—another room
town or even country.
I touch the remote control (I smile) . . .
that's how what we use to call the children –
they were running between the summer games
to buy cigarettes or beer
I'm not falling asleep, deafening crash
click, click
in the tired silence of the sleeping air. I get up
My eyes are searching an opened window
to see people in which they quarrel.

Imprint
Jean Colonomos

A pint-sized six-year-old squirms at the piano
while the teacher instructs her how to play
"Hot Cross Buns,"— a three-note melody
    Preoccupied with ballerina Maria Tallchief,
    who she knows from a photo on a wall
    at her ballet school, she deafens to the notes.

At the end of the third lesson, she overhears the teacher:
Mrs. Roberts, you're wasting your money. Every time
I teach your daughter a tune, she skips off the bench to dance.
    In the picture, Tallchief's head is crowned with
    Swan Lake's iconic white-feathered headband.
    The photo calls out to the girl,
    a lighthouse illuminating curiosity
    where imagination takes the lead.

Monsieur Viznishensky
Jean Colonomos

How valiant we were we ballet brats, the subject of
Monsieur's Mother-Russia depressions.
He'd smack one of us with his cane,
for all to know
       Rasputin was still alive.

Dancers' Mantra
Jean Colonomos

Come to us in class. Sing your sway of **no pain, no gain**
when we place our bulging dance bags under the piano, purses
packed with dance clothes and accessories for the day ahead.
Listen as the Sirens seduce **no pain, no gain** for the next hour and a
half, this looping mantra that makes us dancer-worthy. If backs
spasm, if the skin on the tops of our feet bleed from knee crawls
that mimic stigmata, if a tendon snaps from overstretching, this is
good. Inborn is the need for motion, speed and extremes to create
beauty's illusions. We embrace the **no pain, no gain** bloom of
injuries to reach perfection's ideal.

Photograph - D Ferrara

Something New, Something Strange
Lenore Hart

Halfway up the walk, Jason noticed his mother had decorated the painted-plaster garden gnomes for spring. They stood in the flower border, staring out like ugly little aliens, surrounded by cracked pots of tulips.

At her door he took a deep breath, pulled up his mask, and knocked. After a minute or so he heard the shuffle of slippers. The click-click-clack of three locks turned and unbolted.

The door swung open. In the dusk beyond, her blue-white curls seemed to levitate above the shining rims of her bifocals. "Come on in, honey."

"Hey, Ma. Just dropped by to see . . . where's your mask? Better —"

"I can't breathe with that thing on. Back's too sore to even bend, then I can't hardly get up. But I don't complain."

In the living room he dropped into his father's armchair, snatching a falling doily in mid-fall. Redraped it and glanced at his watch. In about an hour he needed to get back to work. "All that gardening you do. It'll cripple you."

"Little work never hurt nobody. Got to keep things nice."

Jason nodded. "Sure. I suppose."

"Had to slip a note in Jane Trimble's box yesterday. Left her garage door open again. Leaving her mess out for the world to see. She come over and complained. Well, her garage faces the street. A midget couldn't turn around in it."

His mother's face looked flushed, shiny. Her hands twisted in her lap, over and under, like small excited animals.

He insisted on taking her temperature. It was normal, thank God.

"Say. Look, Ma." He put away the thermometer and slipped some brochures from his pocket. "That new retirement place. Private rooms, your own furniture. Raised flower beds. Even people in wheelchairs can garden, no bending. They'd fix all your meals. There's a beauty shop on the premises."

She stared blankly, squinting, nose wrinkled.

He sighed and tossed the brochures on the side table. "I'll leave them. Maybe later."

He sniffed at the air. Was that burning he smelled? Now he saw a thin scarf of smoke was unfurling from the kitchen.

"Mom!" He jumped up. "Were you just cooking?"

She tilted her head. "Was I?"

Jason ran to the kitchen. Flames licked at one burner energetically as a campfire. He grabbed salad tongs and snagged a smoking mess of charcoaled oven mitt. Pitched it underhand into the sink. Inside the cool oven, a pink brick of raw meatloaf sat like dog mess in a Pyrex dish.

His mother wandered in as he was dousing the mitt. Which was easy since the faucet had been running, too.

"You left it on, Ma." His voice shook; it did no good to shout. "Again. Turned the burner on instead of the oven."

She looked shocked. "I never did."

"The water was running, too."

190

She tsked as if this was his fault somehow, and went back to the living room. When Jason came out, she was leafing through Good Housekeeping. Still shaking her head.

"Ma. Listen."

She gasped and dropped the magazine. "Oh! You give me a start."

"You can't live alone here anymore. I put new batteries in the smoke alarms, but . . . it's just too much for you. Someday it'll burn down, with you in it. Then what?"

She smiled as if relieved to have an answer. "Fire insurance is all paid up." She rose and looked around. "Well, I got lots to do. The fellow moved in behind, last year? His old ear tree overhangs my fence. Those nasty black seed pods. Disgrace. And he drinks, too."

He had to get her in to someplace. Though he'd read nursing homes had been hotbeds of COVID infection. There was a vaccine now, of course, but she'd refused to get the shot.

"They shoot little computer chips into you through the needle," she had informed him, when he had offered to set up an appointment with her doctor. "To track everybody like housepets. I heard about it on Fox."

He'd explained why this was not the case, several times. She just shook her head and said cryptically, "I know what I know."

"I'll be back on Tuesday," said Jason, giving up for the moment.

The following week, each gnome wore a jaunty straw hat and had a basket of egg-shaped plastic panty hose containers.

"My God," Jason muttered. "Alien Easter."

He knocked six times, mashed the buzzer. Rattled the screen. Couldn't see, through heavy lace curtains, anything like a sprawled body. Panting, he sprinted around to the side yard. She's fallen in the garden, yanking up carrots and radishes. Impaled on a tomato stake. Jesus . . .

He burst through the box hedge and saw her under the ear tree. Talking nine to the dozen, waving her arms. No mask, of course.

"Ma!" He ducked under the tree and some sort of meteor-shower beaned him. Black pods rained down around him like dried severed ears.

"Hey, Ma. What – "

Across the fence, a fat old man in a Hawaiian shirt, very bald, sat on an upturned milk crate. Smoking a big cigar, ignoring them.

"You gonna trim this thing?" His mother shook a clenched fist. "Or do I send another letter?"

Silence. The man was immobile, but gave off the aura of a dormant volcano. Wreaths of smoke ringed his dome. He wore no mask either, but Jason thought better of pointing this out.

"Ma," he said. "Come inside. Don't get upset." He grasped her elbow. She stared as if she didn't know him.

"So you won't, Mr. Good-For-Nothing-Lazy-Pants?" she spat at the neighbor.

"Ma," Jason stepped in front. "Look. Don't have a heart attack over a tree."

She craned around, as if he were a just big hat blocking her view at the movies. "Fine. I'll do it myself!" Jumping on her own milk crate, she grabbed the thickest limb with both hands. It bowed, then sprang back, swinging her up off the ground. She kicked over the crate, then hung like an angry monkey: thick ankles, thin legs in elastic stockings kicking below a hem of flowered house dress.

"God sakes, Ma!" Jason hauled on her waist, but she clung to the branch like beggar lice. He had to pry each finger off

192

separately. Finally he was able to hustle her off. He glanced back over one shoulder; Vesuvius Man hadn't moved.

Inside, he plopped her on the couch, less gently than he'd meant to. Raked both hands through his hair, which felt somehow electrified. I'm forty-five, he thought. Killer job in advertising. Not a geriatric nurse. What if she gets sick?

"This is the limit, Ma. I'm staying the night. Tomorrow we will check out assisted living places."

His mother brushed leaf-mold off the front of her dress. "Let's have a nice glass of mint tea. Made it this morning." She paused, as if listening to another voice. "Didn't I?"

"Who knows, Ma?" Jason lowered his head, breathed in, then out. In, then out. Stay calm, that's the ticket. Possibilities churned like unsorted laundry. He was being transferred to Tampa in a month. With his live-in girlfriend. The middle of a worldwide pandemic was not exactly the best time to leave a good job, however stressful. Even if he could move in here, he wouldn't be home all day anyway.

He'd hired several companions. She'd fired each one the same day. When the last wouldn't change the channel from *All My Children* to *Jeopardy*, his mother had walloped her with the business end of a broom.

He called the office and took a week of annual leave. Finger-brushed his teeth, afraid to leave her alone even long enough to hit Walgreens for a toothbrush. He slept in a tattered old t-shirt of his father's she must've been using as a dust rag. Its lemon oil reek kept him awake long after his mother's deep, even breathing became snores.

Sometime later he jolted awake. His mother was standing over his bed, screaming. The flash and glitter in her waving hand grabbed his attention. A wicked slice of moonlight.

A fucking butcher knife.

Jason shot up, slammed back against the headboard. "Jesus on a pony, Ma. What the hell?"

She stared out the window over his bed. "Bastard!" she shrieked. "Crazy-ass son of a bitch!"

Jason hadn't even realized she knew those words. She'd never spoken a swear stronger than "I Suwannee" throughout his childhood and adolescence. Each curse was punctuated with a dull thud . . . thud . . . thud from outside, as if God were playing rap music at 16 rpm.

He stood on the mattress. Grabbed her knife hand and disarmed her. Wrenched the blinds apart, and saw a huge green bomb hurtling at his face.

"Shit!" He threw himself flat onto the mattress. When he finally looked up, his mother's expression was that of a righteous woman.

"See? Old fart's been drinking. He's throwing them at the house again."

Thud.

"Throwing?" said Jason. "Who?"

In the mirror hung on the back of the door, he was panting, wide-eyed, like a war refugee. Oh my God, I'll lose it, too, he thought. After a few days of this—

Thud.

"I sent a letter." She folded her arms and smiled.

Enough. He rushed out the back door, not caring he wore only boxers and a dust rag. The backyard was empty, but there came the thud of a door slamming, somewhere beyond the fence. Under the back bedroom window lay a pile of broken watermelons leaking their pink watery guts into the ivy.

"Tomorrow morning," he muttered. "Assisted living. As God is my witness."

When he came in, his mother was in the kitchen, frying chops. Maybe a dozen. In two pans. "Afraid these'll go bad," she said, cheerfully flipping away.

"By morning?"

The pork sizzled sullenly, slowly turning to leather.

Jason took hold of her shoulder and turned her around. "Ma."

She held the spatula stiffly, like a flyswatter at port arms, refusing to answer.

"It's three a.m. Still dark. Even the paperboy's asleep."

"Let me go," she said testily. "I got to cook these up. A sin to waste good food."

"Ma." He about-faced her, confiscated the spatula, and they marched down the hall. "Get in bed. Please. Tomorrow we have an appointment."

"Let go my arm." She turned on him, teeth bared. "Why don't you just let go? Let me die in peace?" Her voice was low, guttural. Hateful. Her glasses, sitting crooked on the bridge of her nose, winked moonlight at him. Round, opaque. Alien eyes.

He felt a chill. Who is this woman? he thought. She's not my mother. Not anymore. She's going to ruin the rest of my life.

"Get out of my house!" she shouted.

He laughed. "Sure, Ma. Then maybe someday I can die in peace, too." He kept on pushing her steadily toward the bed. Not hard or fast, but at the edge she collapsed like a ragdoll on the rumpled quilt. He saw it all reflected in the trifold vanity across the room.

When he was little, she'd always sat there to brush her hair and carefully apply beautiful poppy-red lipstick. Once when he was about four he'd sneaked in and gotten the golden tube out. A few strokes later and he'd seen reflected in the three mirrors a ghastly painted midget, bloody-faced, stranger than the garden gnomes.

Which had frightened him back then, especially after dark. He'd rubbed at his face, shrieking and crying.

His mother had rushed in and picked him up, ignoring the expensive mashed lipstick. "There now," she'd said, kissing his face. "You'll be okay. Don't cry, honey, please." She'd kissed his face and gotten out a lace-edged hanky, smiling at him in the mirror as she fixed everything.

Now all he saw reflected there was an angry, disheveled man standing over an old woman with tears streaking her face.

What are we all becoming? he thought. Something new. Something strange.

He reached out and pulled a tissue from the nightstand box. "There now, Ma," he said softly, leaning over to gently wipe her face.

Then he put his arms around her. "We'll be okay. Please, please, honey. Don't cry."

Action Figure
Butterfly Thomas

A little me
I can see you
Doing the things I used to do
Saying the things I used to say
You will go further than I, in your life, I pray
You'll be greater than I am today
Take action
Figure it out
Mini me
I can see
Your desire for autonomy
Mistakes will be made
As you learn your way
Reflect and pray
And you'll be okay
Sit still
Or don't
Explore
Learn more
Do more

Take action
As you figure life out
Child of mine
Daughter divine
Talk to me
I'm here for you
Or to your village
They're here too
Young activist
If you insist
If you must
Fight for what's fair
Fight for what's just
Grow into yourself
Into who you are
Into who you will be
Then we'll all see
What you're about
As you take action
And figure life out

Baby Boy
Butterfly Thomas

Baby boy
My love my joy
I see you
Growing up too
Fast for me
Oh the agony
The pain
The pride
In watching you
Try to do what you need to
To have a good life
Remember as you get older
I still want to hold your
Hand give you hugs
Show you love
I'll be here when you trip when you stumble
When you're praised when you're humbled
As you find your way
As you make mistakes
By your side, I'll stay

Here, I'll be
Cause you came from me
So remember as we enjoy
Each other's antics and excitement
Even when you annoy
Me or despite it
You're always my baby boy

Questions
Butterfly Thomas

Can I ask you a question
My love
My dear?
Are you open
To listen
To hear?
Where are you going
This month
This year?
Can you slow down
To experience
To revere?
Express your emotions
A laugh
A tear
You have your whole life
Waiting
My dear
Just a few questions
A couple of suggestions...

To be clear
Don't lose yourself
Improve yourself
Try not to veer
Off course
Cause you're a force
In which to be reckoned
Listen a second
Do you know what to do
When distraction appears?
When obstacles draw near?
When it gets to be too much?
When you don't feel as tough?
When you want to give up?
I'm here...
I'm here

War Reporter
Colin Pink

I often wonder why I do it. Go to war zones. Report on war zones. I'm often asked. I say, someone's got to do it. Someone has to show what's going on. But I know that isn't the truth. I have to go.

I have to witness human beings at the extremes, on the point of breaking, there, at that point, where something extraordinary happens. Something you never see anywhere else.

The tea is passed and the cup rattles in my hand. Outside the mortars land and jets shriek. We talk.

I never spoke to my parents. Not through some adolescent annoyance but because they were dead before I attained the power of speech.

It's funny never knowing someone so close. When do they feel part of you and when do they not? They were always just out of reach like a word I can't remember.

War separates families.

We convince ourselves we tell people about something urgent. Something they need to know. Shoehorned between the economy and the weather on the evening news. I often ask myself, am I helping these people or am I just helping myself to their lives?

A man opens his mouth in pain. His lips peel back as if his teeth are trying to climb out of his mouth.

In the mall the children practice being consumers. A delivery man drops a heavy package with a bang. I duck. The children laugh.

Another shell lands nearby and a fine coating of plaster dust settles on the tea. My host offers me sugar.

I am just a visitor. I am in it but not of it. I can go back home. But for them, for them they are home already. When I go I leave behind those who have no other place to go—minus their stories.

I'm running into an alleyway escaping the *zing zing zing* of a street that's jumping with the hornet stings of small arms fire. I'm running into the arms of parents I never knew who vanish at every embrace. There's smoke everywhere.

After every trip I say to myself, that's it, that's the last. No more. But, after a while, things get stale and I get that itchy feeling, like I'm missing out on something. I want to pack a bag and be packing a reason for going.

The shelling stops. The air is full of dust. It reminds me of builders. That dry smell, constricted throat. Walls torn down. Brick dust. Plaster dust. In the distance a siren.

You can't tell anyone anything. They have to find out for themselves. Sometimes I stand looking into a butcher's window at the choice cuts of meat. In an eyeblink I'm gazing down into the gutted interior of an armoured personnel carrier. Bits of leg, thigh, shoulder, thick cuts.

In St. Bride's church, just off Fleet Street, there's a side chapel with name cards on the altar of journalists who have been killed in the line of duty. Little flickering candles sit among the names. Silent truths slowly going out.

Sometimes I just want to scoop them up, pick them up, gather them into my arms and run. Just run with them. And keep on running.

I'm adept at getting across borders. I speak the language of borders. I'm used to the ways of borders, their habits, quirks, prejudices. I find my way across. I'm always crossing over.

Everyone else has a family. Not having one myself always felt like something important I had somehow neglected to do.

At the checkpoint they look at my papers. Gun pointing. Casual. They look me up and down, face, clothes, boots. I notice I walk differently when the guns are pointing. Self-conscious. More contained. Careful to move slowly.

My parents live in a place over the border. Impossible to find. Always slipping out of sight every time I turn my head. But sometimes, when I listen to music, I think I can hear them, slipped between the notes, like a ticket left inside a book.

You can't get the smell of mass graves out of your nostrils. You can't get the smell of mass graves onto the evening news. But I'd like to.

The tracer drifts into the night sky like a kite set free. Flaming fists streaming upwards only to vanish.

There are holes in the walls of the hotel from the previous day's shelling. But there are still rooms. Though no running water.

I can't show most of what I see. Conventions. There are conventions about what it is acceptable to show. You wouldn't want to put people off their evening meal. Pass the salt.

The laptop screen shines. There's another email, fat with attachments, sitting in my inbox. It smells like another assignment. Another catastrophe calling.

My bag is packed. I'm waiting on the border between the living and the dead. Pointing both ways. Unable to decide which way to turn.

Laughing And Grief
Rosie Johnston

This is the meal I came for: *suprême de volaille* with *dauphinoises* followed by chocolate mousse on shortbread with a marinated pear and two swirls of jus. Now cognac. Through the window's gold lettering, the street is drying in sunlight. It's been a proper Parisian meal, all understated expertise, not a vegetable in sight, and here winding through the exuberant voices comes my *café crème*.

My coat is still damp on the empty chair across my table, and I toast it as if it's my father. He adored Europe and hauled us all as teenagers to campsites the length and breadth of it. Our Irish island could never contain my dad any more than a conventional marriage could.

In my memory's caverns, he's holding my baby brother over his head singing "Say goodbye now to pastimes and play, lad." As if he were singing to his own unmarried self, though he loved being a father. Ah yes, *The Marriage of Figaro*. My father in a frock coat measuring for his bridal bed while parents from our school strolled around him in wigs and brocade singing too. I was forty before I realised my mother sent me to those rehearsals with colouring books—the only child there—to remind him, and everybody else, he was a Belfast teacher with a wife and kids.

In my bag, my phone buzzes. Emails started piling up the minute I settled in the Eurostar, and before I'd made it through the Gare du Nord crowds, there were hundreds. I've ignored them all: these three days are ruthlessly scheduled for me. Me alone.

I feel the warmth of you here now, Dad. Or it might be the cognac. I was away on a literary trail to Montparnasse this morning. To find Beckett. Inside the cemetery gates, with rain coming on, I did my best to memorise the notice showing who was where, and off I went. In the February light, the cemetery had the look of a monochrome ocean floor designed on graph paper. Sections grew into and over each other in a jumble of beached mausoleums and headstones adrift among lichen and moss.

It should have been easy. I couldn't miss Maupassant's memorial for example, surely. A big, fuck-off thing with white railings and his name on a pediment in capitals but could I find it? *Non.* I pounded around where Beckett was supposed to be. Nothing obviously him so I trawled down the narrow tracks between the graves, then the same exercise crosswise. So many families. So much money spent—one particularly fancy vault was dedicated to 'Famille de Bully' and here was I, ignoring them all for a playwright. Had I strayed into one of his plays? Not so much *Waiting for Godot* as *Searching for the Great Man*. Would he ever appear? Would it make any sense if he did?

You would have known where he was, Dad. I longed to phone you, like that time in Edinburgh. I could feel Mr Hyde scampering up every shadowy side-street but where was Stevenson himself? You answered my call immediately, as always, and told me how Stevenson, his wife and the dog, all of them perpetually unwell, moved to Eastern Samoa for the good of their health. Until, at the age of only forty-four, Stevenson died there of an aneurism pulling the cork from a bottle of exceptional red. It was the exit you'd hoped for yourself.

I was about to go when I heard a voice: "Vous cherchez quelqu'un?"

A small man in his eighties stood there, his eyes all gentleness when he smiled, all loneliness when he didn't. He was Henri, he said, lived close by. With droplets shining on his black overcoat, scarf and large sheepskin gloves, he was oblivious to what had turned to sleet, even when drips hung from his nose and earlobes. He guided me the few paces to Beckett's plain granite slab, unmissable on the main path, with a single pot of heather. In exactly the right section.

Had I seen the others, Henri asked. There wasn't another living soul around us. "Suivez-moi."

Sleet draped lace everywhere and together our steps melted Henri's single line of footsteps. He walked with a geriatric shuffle, pointing to a famous grave here or there—Baudelaire, Saint-Saens—until one of the huge gloves slid loose and dropped at his feet. He bent painfully, refusing help, tucked it into his coat and slid both his hands into the other one. He wobbled his thumbs around in their narrow space as if he were making a rabbit shadow on a wall, grinning: "Plus chaud comme cela." I could see exactly what sort of little boy he'd been.

Parisian *amour* for their flawed celebrities clearly survives *la mort*. Memorabilia at Chirac's grave included fruit, toys, baskets of violets left by grandchildren perhaps, or mistresses. Serge Gainsbourg sang about some metro station or other so tourists ask at the station if they can keep their tickets and leave them, each with a pebble on top, for Serge. The joint grave for De Beauvoir and Sartre is glorious pink marble covered in red and coral lipstick kisses. Defiant French kisses.

Gravel crunched behind us; we were no longer alone. A hundred feet away an elegant young Chinese woman in a black face mask and trench coat sauntered along the central promenade, eyes only for her phone. Nothing remarkable there except for four soldiers in square formation around her, also in masks, their rifles cocked and ready. At the gates, they swung left onto the street.

She mesmerised me. Her structured solitude, as if she carried a fortress around her more visibly than I did. Was she from Wuhan, was this her isolation? I didn't have a face mask. Should I get one?

A nudge at my elbow was Henri guiding me again. There was agitation in his shuffle as we approached a plain grave near the exit. Pebbles traced out a heart shape and in the middle under a white stone was a laminated Valentine's card. Jean Seberg, 1938-1979.

Henri stood and bent his bare head. His hands, still together in their single glove, met under his chin as if in prayer.

I had no idea who she was or how this beautiful American with a stack of Hollywood films to her credit had such impact here in Paris. Henri explained, tears lighting his eyes: her marriages, her so-called suicide, the FBI's apology for hounding her, her tragedy.

"We are nothing more than dust and shadow," he muttered in French.

"Horace," I said. My father taught Classics—Laughing and Grief, as the Mock Turtle used to say—and read, talked, joked so much in Latin, my mother forbade it anywhere near her. He yielded eventually, saying he would be thankful not to be *persona non grata* in his own home.

Henri beamed, folded away his single glove and lifted my hand in its fitted black leather into his own. How he had enjoyed spending time with someone "jeune et jolie," he said, and slowly pressed his lips to my gloved knuckles. We had spoken in nothing but French so far, he politely accepting my efforts, correcting nothing. Now he spoke in English, Dryden's English:

> *Happy the man, and happy he alone,*
> *He who can call today his own:*
> *He who, secure within, can say*
> *Tomorrow, do thy worst, for I have lived today'*

Dear Henri. His flawless courtesy forbade him to acknowledge or even notice how his words breached the crackling force of my seclusion, and the emotional collapse I did my best to hide. Within a handful of seconds, I was immersed in hospital again with you in ICU after that catastrophic operation. The silent nurse at her station, the array of tubes and contraptions, that racking cough that turned you Dickensian puce until you reached for me, my hand, and gripped it until the worst subsided. I creamed your arthritic hands and feet when they flaked, brought you recordings of Figaro and Susanna, read to you —read to you time and again your favourite poet. From your favourite Ode—3, 29: *Happy the Man.*

In those few seconds at Seberg's grave, I am kissing your forehead again on that last night of your breathing, as everything you knew ebbed away. I am at your graveside in heartless winds during what was always going to be a complicated funeral; so many good-looking senior women who knew you so well, each taking a quiet moment to confide with me, "Carpe diem." Orphaned, stranded, I marveled at your talent for welcoming love.

My mother hated that talent of course. "There are worse things than being single," she used to say, trying to understand my office life. But she was not the parent who loved me. That was you, my father, who first held me while she was stitched and tended, while she nursed her own resentment of me for being female. But you, Dad, your promise to me resounded then in the deepest whorls of my ears, a promise made to my child hand resting in yours, to my child eyes and ears experiencing an orchestra for the first time, to my heart when you gave me my first copy of Heaney. Remember that day you were driving us all the length of France and saw peaches for sale at the roadside? "Let's get peaches," you shouted, "let's get a whole tray!"

Henri allowed my hand to belong to me again and bent for the card on Seberg's grave to show me. *Jamais de désespoir*, it said inside, in elderly French script. From you, I asked. More a blink than a nod told me, yes.

I have thought of Henri often over the past year. He was the last man to kiss me before we lurched into this world of lockdowns, solitude, panic, one crisis after another, lost opportunities, grief. What are the odds he's still breathing? Whose was the last face he saw before they closed the ambulance door and that world of masked smiles and vinyl kindness absorbed him? Who held his hand? Who read him Horace, whispered *nil desperandum*?

We shook hands like the strangers we were, and it wasn't until I was out and beyond the crossing that I was awash with tears.

Any restaurant would do, I had to eat and, eyes wiped, I pushed into one with red window frames and gold lettering. After that meal, with cognac and *café crème* beside me, I opened my wire-topped journal and began to scribble my way into some sense in all this. When my fingers were exhausted, I leant back and rested my eyes on the sun setting golden at the end of the street.

"It's time, darling."

Your voice, for me alone.

"It's time to let go now, and live."

A breath came out of me, something like joy. I paid for my meal and walked out into the evening's glitter back towards the

212

Seine. There was a new swing in my walk, unfamiliar strength. Whatever came my way back home, I was going to welcome it. Like father, like daughter, I would live my life to the full and embrace love.

It's not been as easy as that, of course. I work from home now, part-time, and help at the food bank. My hair is looser, my heels flatter and though I have less money in the bank, I'm richer than I've ever been. I'm saving to come back to Montparnasse cemetery where I will sit down by Jean Seberg's grave with a bottle of exceptional red and read Horace until Henri comes.

If Henri does not come, I will leave a message of hope for Jean Seberg anchored by a white stone.

Jamais de désespoir.

Never lose hope.

Missing - Carol MacAllister

The Night Cleaner
Mona D. Miller

She showed up when most of the lawyers had cleared out, even the gung-ho litigators who were there until ten every night. Pale, middle-aged, wearing the agency's white coat with the blue lettering. "Vivian." Seemed like a frivolous name for a woman pushing a cart with a huge trash bin, cleaning materials, rags, stuff. She was very solid-looking. And sad, too. He didn't know exactly what was bothering her, but it seemed clear she was not leading a happy life.

Most people ignored her. A few people said "Hi, Vivian," before jumping on the elevator for the ride down from the 35th floor. He'd worked late enough times to have seen her in his own office, not just the hallways. She'd politely ask if it was okay to come in, take the wastepaper basket from under his desk without touching his legs (not easy, because he was tall), replace it, emptied, gently wipe the pale wood credenza, and disappear before he had time to look up from the motion he was writing. He often looked at the paper rather than have to dwell on her face. "I will come later, Mister," she'd say, in her strange accent, gesturing to the commercial vacuum cleaner that rode shotgun with the bin. She never vacuumed if someone was inside an office.

Now, hiding in the upstairs war room, full of boxes of documents and trial notebooks, he wished he'd never talked to her. He was lying on the floor with his mistress, who also worked on the case. They'd already shed a lot of their clothes with considerable enthusiasm when they'd heard the vacuum heading their way. It stopped them cold.

They were both married, their affair was totally against at least seven different firm policies, and nobody knew. Was Vivian going to be the one who found out? The night cleaner? It seemed preposterous. But he'd volunteered to help Vivian with an immigration problem, once. And she'd mentioned her son, too. Could she possibly be looking for him? At one A.M.?

Not possible. This was a nightmare.

The lights were out. "We could lock the door," whispered Greta.

"She probably has a master key."

They both began to giggle, imagining what it would look like to Vivian to open the door and discover them hiding under the conference table. They covered their mouths so nobody would hear.

Vivian passed the frosted glass door and kept going. She pushed the vacuum cleaner as hard as she could. It was heavy. But it wouldn't do to embarrass the man, whatever he was doing in that room. She'd come back later. She couldn't afford to make any trouble.

Isla Verde
David R. Brubaker

I've consumed over a thousand Nutri-Grain soft baked breakfast bars from Kellogg's since the beginning of the pandemic. I've also devoured more than three hundred packs of Marchan Ramen Noodle Soup ("cooks in three minutes"), and over six hundred bananas during the past year, not to mention nearly fifteen hundred Diet Cokes. This is an extreme version of my normal diet, a by-product of COVID-19 crisis that has rendered me increasingly lethargic.

The only clothing I've bought during the past year is a pair of discounted sneakers on Amazon, and our bills for gas and tolls have been minimal—we've driven less than 2,000 miles. The only uptick in costs is that I've ordered more books online than usual, and the piles next to my chair have grown exponentially. I don't bother to go to stores anymore. Cat food running low? Amazon. Ink cartridge needs to be replaced? Amazon. I don't bother with very much at all; I languish in the psychological swamp of COVID-19.

My life has become "Groundhog Day." I awaken at 8:34 AM, go downstairs to prepare my coffee, grab a bar or two, and sit down in front of my computer to check the pre-market for stocks and peruse Facebook, and Amazon. Then I scan the *Philadelphia Inquirer, Washington Post, Wall Street Journal, South China Morning Post, Manila Bulletin* and *USA Today,* all online, before heading out with my wife Marilyn for a three-mile walk along a route that rarely changes. When I return home, I work for two or three hours on a course I am teaching, my writing, or some issue with the Lititz Borough Council. Then I take another walk with my beloved, maybe a couple of miles. Then I check my email and stock market closing prices, have a healthy dinner prepared by Marilyn and watch the news. If it were not for her, I'd probably have a bowl of cereal or order a pizza. Then I read a little, take a shower, and we figure out what to watch on Netflix. Every day...every day. Sure, there are interruptions: Zoom meetings of all sorts, or, perhaps, something to sign for or a scam call, or perhaps a FaceTime call from my children.

You see, we're used to traveling eight weeks of the year, often to Southeast Asia, but this has not been possible during the outbreak. We've been at home. My teaching (four courses in the past year), and my local government meetings have been on Zoom. I feel a little guilty. I should be reading more, be more productive. I could clean out the attic or garage, yet they remain untouched. I wonder how many others are like us during the pandemic. It's hard to know. Hopefully, things will improve. Courses and meetings will return to normal, and we'll have interactions in person with actual people. Then again...

One benefit of this past year is that we've accumulated money, and the stock and housing markets have boomed. Our account balances have climbed, and psychologically we feel more secure, although we understand that the economy can change quickly. I wonder about those who have lost jobs, lost businesses. What about industries being destroyed? What will the future look like and how long will COVID-19 have such an impact on our lives?

Recently I said to Marilyn, "screw it…let's go to Puerto Rico. We've been vaccinated. Let's just go."

The chango, formally the Greater Antillean grackle, nonchalantly landed on our outdoor breakfast table, gave us a wink, and used its razor-sharp beak to poke a small hole in one of the jelly packets about six inches from my right hand. After slurping about a quarter of its contents, the shiny black bird gave us a mocking glance and flew off into the tropical environs. It seemed that not much had changed in Isla Verde, an affluent enclave near San Juan with a world-class beach, five minutes from the airport, always in the low eighties with a strong breeze. The ebony birds—gregarious, loud, and always hungry—were endemic to the area, boldly working the beach crowd for morsels of lunches, and flocking to outdoor restaurants whose patrons routinely either encouraged or ignored them.

After a year of COVID-19 sequestration, we wondered how the area had fared. After all, Puerto Rico had just been through a debt crisis and bankruptcy in 2016, and two major hurricanes, Irma, and Maria, in 2017, which had caused horrendous devastation to the island. We'd escaped our home for our annual five-night beach vacation, continuous since 2002, save for 2020, and, at first, the changes we noticed were minor. Our flight was, as usual, packed, and the chaos at both the Philadelphia and San Juan airports was reminiscent of previous trips, except for the paperwork, COVID-19 tests, masks, and ubiquitous hand sanitizer and temperature machines.

Business was picking up, and Jodi, the receptionist at the hotel Villa Del Sol, said that "It's like Christmas," with extended families returning home for vacations, and travelers arriving from the states. "We're pretty full," she said, "I think we're getting back to normal. This past year has been awful." Lupi's Mexican Grill and

Sports Cantina, around the corner, seemed busy, as expected. The outdoor seating was packed, although we noticed that there weren't many people dining inside.

One reason I come to Isla Verde is to purchase smoking pipes and supplies. I'm a Savinelli man and I prefer a strong Latakia blend in a fine Italian pipe, one of my only luxuries. Mohamad, my supplier, operates a small souvenir shop on Ave. Isla Verde, and I visit him every year. He knows what I like, and he understands the products he sells. I wondered if he had survived the recent turmoil and found that he had. "Business is picking up," he said, "I think things will be alright," he said. While he didn't have any pipe tobacco, I was able to purchase a couple beauties from him, and was impressed that he seemed upbeat, even while relating his usually negative litany of news about the goings-on in the area.

Walking around Isla Verde, we noticed that the upscale hotels and condo buildings had largely been repaired, a major change from last time, right after the hurricanes. In 2019, our last visit, we saw windows blown out, wall panels missing, and general destruction, even to the most expensive buildings. Although the Ritz-Carlton remained closed, the Marriott, the Fairmont El San Juan, and the Royal Sonesta were all restored and operational, and long-established family restaurants with a strong, local clienteles also were doing relatively well. At first glance, things appeared almost normal.

But when you looked closer, you'd see the damage caused by the exodus from the island, the permanent destruction of seemingly perpetual catastrophe. For example, the Sweet Bakery was the kind of place where Dad would prepare your hotcakes while Mom rang you up, where customers' photographs dotted the walls, and folks took their pictures with the giant beach float. In was a basic place with good home-cooked food at a fair price, and a distinctly quirky, home-style atmosphere. We loved it there, but now it was gone. Mohamed told us that "they didn't have enough capital to hold on, they couldn't withstand the hurricane and the virus. I heard they went to the States." Their store is still vacant, now vandalized. There are businesses like this up and down Ave. Isla Verde, between the condo buildings. Like the ice cream parlor and the bank branch, the bagel shop, and the Chinese restaurant, they are gone forever, replaced by establishments selling medicinal marijuana or nothing at all. The domed nightclub is gone, too, covered with artistic graffiti,

Photograph - David R. Brubaker

something traditionally verboten in Isla Verde. These were family shops that are not apt to return, their proprietors broke and dispersed.

If you walk up and down Ave. Isla Verde at night, you will find it surreal. We arrived on a Friday evening and went for a walk.

This once-hyperkinetic boulevard was empty of people, with businesses closed and only a few cars passing us by. It took us a couple of blocks to realize that the town had instituted a COVID-19 related curfew (from ten at night to five in the morning) and we needed to get back to the hotel. During the day, folks mainly stayed away from the avenue unless they were making a CVS or pizza run, and police officers stopped you to remind you to wear your mask. The fine for first offenders was $250, the second $500 and the third offense meant big trouble. The bus system, always erratic at best, was in chaos. With limited COVID seating, buses filled quickly and passed you by as you waited for a ride. You could wait for hours, maybe all day, for a bus to let you in, and unless you had the money for one of the few cabs still around, you were stuck in place.

Wide expanses of beach at Isla Verde were lightly populated, and the ubiquitous chair-and-umbrella vendors harder to find. The beach hawkers had disappeared, but the smells and sounds of the sea were intact. It was impossible to find food nearby, and half-empty beachfront hotels wouldn't admit you to their premises to buy food and drink or use the facilities. I wondered what happened to workers who were displaced by the pandemic. Sure, they'd get a little COVID-19 relief, but their payments were delayed for months because all funds were passed through the dysfunctional Puerto Rican government. Many lived in the nearby San Juan Luis Llorens Torres Residential complex, a public housing development recently housing about 2900 souls. After the hurricanes, where many died, the survivors, at least those who could, simply abandoned their apartments and left the island for good. Until recently, there has been no running water or electricity, no telephone or Internet, no protection from the tropical heat amidst the ruin. COVID-19 created another exodus, but many stayed put with no alternative. The complex, the largest public housing project in Puerto Rico (located in the nearby San Juan neighborhood of Santurce), had been decimated and criminalized—it was a dangerous place, unlike Isla Verde with its high tax base and vigorous police presence.

I thought that maybe Isla Verde was an allegory of what has happened throughout the world. After all, while condo rentals were down, prices were up, and insurance paid much of the cost to reconstruct damaged properties. The usual fleet of Maseratis and Porsches seemed intact, and the upscale hotels were doing a brisk business, even if the casinos seemed thin. The affluent were doing well, despite the events of recent years.

The poor were bearing a disproportionate share of the suffering. With limited incomes, and an increasingly problematic job market, they were being forced to live in abhorrent conditions with little income. Those with relatives in the United States, and some money, could leave the island. Those left behind had little recourse, and, until late April 2021, few vaccinations.

The Ritz-Carlton will soon reopen, returned to better than its former glory, ready to receive customers willing to pay $500 per night. The poor will remain poor, and the return of their service jobs will help, but not nearly enough for a decent life. The project will remain dangerous and under-policed, and as folks eventually find their way to places like Florida. will be replaced with prosperous retirees and larger condominium communities.

There is a new algorithm to life now, a Darwinian calculation that serves to protect society's "winners." In a few months, the casinos and posh hotels will be back to business-as-usual, capitalizing on the beauty of the ocean, the wide pristine beaches, breezy Caribbean climate, and the ease with which those from the states can come here. They will exploit the commons, the natural environment held by us all. It'll be a cash cow. Affluent retirees and distance-working professionals will flock here and will make the State of Puerto Rico a mecca of a tropical paradise, offering Caribbean amenities at relatively affordable prices. There will be a building boom, with new casinos, hotels and condo buildings constructed on every available parcel. There'll be fine restaurants and upscale shopping.

It'll be great, won't it?

Karma
Monique Antonette Lewis

Wes, an old college friend of Tera's, posted pictures of his wedding on Facebook. During their senior year in college, Wes and Tera were invited to dinner at the home of a couple from the church they attended. The husband was Mexican and his wife white. Three little brown girls surrounded them. Just before the blessing, the husband grabbed his wife's hand and thanked everyone for coming to their home.

"I want to find someone to be completely happy with like that," Wes had told Tera. "Look at them. They're genuinely happy."

Clicking through Wes' photos, Tera can tell from the look in their eyes that they are indeed in love.

"Every time I see someone's wedding pictures or engagement announcements, I'm reminded of what I almost had," Tera tells Leilani on their lunch walk through Washington Park.

"Are you serious? With David!"

"No, that's not what I meant. It just reminds me of what it felt like to be engaged. Although I'm glad it didn't happen, I'm sad it didn't happen. Not that it didn't happen with him, but that I didn't get married at all. That I'm not like the others."

"You talk as if your life is already over. You still have time. You're only 33."

"I'm just sad that I know what that commitment feels like and I wish I never experienced it."

Leilani stops walking and faces Tera. "You just wish you never experienced it with a cheater."

"Well, eventually everyone gets what's coming to them. That makes me feel better."

"You truly believe that, Tera?"

"Yes."

"Humpf. There are some people who I look at and think to myself, where's the mother-fuckin' karma?"

Entombment
Dale Bailes

You who complain of being trapped
In the coffin of your car, imagine
That sound of the lumbering train
Rumbling across the ceiling full-bore
Rocking your bed in morning darkness
As house pets flee through an open
Window, your mattress bounced
From under, then back over, your
Fragile form. A glad protection,
This human sandwich, for when the
Ceiling surely collapses on you.

All this in the time it takes to read these words.

Or is this your mother's fear
Of being buried alive come true?
What searcher through the rubble-
Soon-to-be would think to look

Between the mattress and the springs
For your cold corpse?
And if the house should burn...

That thought propels escape.

Balanced on the wibble-wobble floor
Almost dodge that burl oak dresser
Dancing toward your knees.
Come on. Hobble to the front door.
Blocked. Bookcase and books
Dumped on the floor.
That bedroom window? Jammed.
This other—watch for broken glass.

There is a leap here. Take it.

Across the street, six floors
Of building collapsed into three.
On all sides, cacophony
Of car alarms and barking dogs.
How did we get here
Me naked under a street light?

You can turn away for a second.

A stranger even now has draped
A blanket over me, tells me to
Breathe, breathe deep.
Look, I will be okay now I think.
Go back to what you were about.
But listen, there are always aftershocks.
Let this be a lesson to you.
If your world should crumble,
As worlds are prone to do,
Don't get buried under. Break out.
Breathe deep.
Breathe!

Thistle - Kevin Oderman

Apologetic Doggerel for a Plague Year (#1)
Michael Penny

It's clear no one knows
what to tell me right now
as pandemic wind blows
and no one knows how

to cure it, or tell where it ends.
We're left with suspicions
that no one knows the trends
not the least ignorant politicians

corrupt systems put in place.
Or was it all us foolish
blinded by greed and race
electing these men so toolish?

It's clear no one knows.
Whether it's weather forecasters
who are never right about snows
or historians scanning the past for

details of how we got where we are.
Now, more than ever, we worry
about the direction and how far
we're going—we will be sorry.

Hive
Jo Angela Edwins

In this age stories fall every day from the sky,
and this one falls often—the loss of the bees.

What must it be like to be one of a species
shrinking without knowledge of withering numbers?
Who am I, after all, to assume their ignorance?

I read yesterday the story of a queen
trapped in the crevices of a sedan.
Her workers swarmed the moving car's rear window
and would not leave. Imagine the driver's terror

or wonder. Imagine a species held in thrall
to such a chemical devotion. How could it drift
into the maw of danger? Or is the question how instead
could it not? There are those who number clinging
among the leading causes of early death.

Along the wall between my neighbor's yard and mine
grows mandevilla, a lovely tendrilled vine

with showy flowers. I plant it every year,
as it won't return. The bees have their wild way
with the flowers' deep hollows, then buzz as on a wire
to groundlings, purple phlox or dandelion.

I can think, if I care to, of those I've spent my best
to protect, only to watch them spread their wings
for indifferent attentions from those who might be found
lingering, bored, on any busy corner.
Ask any bee: what attracts may be good or bad,
but at least you'll know the feeling. There lies the queen
beneath three hundred bodies, unseen, dependent,

who knows without knowing she'll never be let go.

Numb
Jo Angela Edwins

Hold a limb in place too long
and lose all feeling.

Watch the digits move thickly but of
their own accord, fat little snakes.

Slice a thumb or pinky toe
and bleed without pain, at least for an instant—

trickle or spurt, ribbon or rhythm
of heartbeat. Is its manic jazz slowed

in your sleepy stillness? Press
a tissue to the wound as the ache returns,

slow as ice melting, slow as breath
losing touch with its reason for being.

Pain, that backwards sword, begins
life dull, sharpening only
after the blood lets go.

Pandemic Dream: My Late Mother's Dream Self Disappears Again
Jo Angela Edwins

but this time I find her
impersonating a newborn baby
in the maternity ward of the hospital
where she worked before I was born.
She is small and swaddled in tea towels,
a tiny cap on her bald head,
but the moment I speak she becomes her adult self,
her sick adult self, also hairless, ducking into a door
on the oncology ward, and I follow and ask
in my disgruntled teacher voice, *Where have you been?*
Why did you disappear again?

I didn't want to worry you, she says, her face
a dark roadmap of stifled anxiety,
and I say as if I were the mother, *Don't you*
understand I was terrified I'd lost you for good
again? She sits on the cold gray vinyl
of the hospital chair, folds her hands that suddenly
are young and unblemished. I've never seen them so,

so I check her face again to be sure she's not gone,
and she isn't. She whispers, *Leukemia.*

In this dream, there is hope in that word,
as I know this is not the cancer that kills her,
so I say, *You will beat this.*
So I say, *Can I stay?*

And she lets me. She looks thin, and I want
to hold her and feed her. I know my touch
will make her flesh mud, so I sit across
the room as we wait for the doctors,
singing together the lullaby she sang to me,
words repeated like birdsong—
nighty, nighty, nighty,
full and warm, my baby doll.

Photograph - David R. Brubaker

Signs
Joel Savishinsky

There are people looking for signs,
those blunt instruments that
stand for themselves, but they
are searching without imagination,
as if the curving arabesques of
bird wings, or the arc of rainbows,
were the Biblical default.

Inside, they find tokens of grace and
election at every turn of the dial,
while the outside is constantly scanned
in a vigilance for the voices that seem
to have fled from the head.

After the breakdown of the reason machine,
the unknowns sold us the salvation of
algorithms and the de-naturing
of nature, foreshadowing what,
in the future, a person will finally
start to glimpse of their past suffering.

But today you can drive down
your freedom road and learn
that all the street signs were
made in prisons.

Binge Watching
Joel Savishinsky

You've watched your fill.
you're hungry still—
just empty shells
of Pavlov's pixels

Photograph - Jeff Talarigo

Joan of Arc Cuts Her Hair for God and Country
Richard Holinger

The nearly silent scissors snip the last few tendrils.

They alight on bare shoulders like warm snowflakes, falling gentle and soft as the words the Lord left her startled with, starting when thirteen as she went about her farmyard chores where she learned of life's suffering, along with nature's beauty. He offers the world to help it endure the worst.

Of victory at Orleans she's assured, not only due her chastity and rejection of marriage (giving herself to Him only), but those who wait for her outside this inn, believers in a virgin sent by God who will sway the local magistrate, especially when he sees a woman turned man willing to face the most humiliating shame a woman can imagine, her sacrifice of warm, valleyed femininity for man's frozen, craggy climes.

Who would displace the loose-fitting gown, so easy on her arms and legs, for skin-scratching pantaloons and prickly shirt, coarse and needled as horsehair that linen shirt and braies cannot shield from scarring?

Not that she needs her former self, the self that curtsied to power.

Even if it means to don the mask and costume of victor, this one will be victorious sans beard, growl, or member to lead her into battle. She will go instead with God, lance enough, shield enough, sword enough, helmet enough to take down enemies reliant only on armor, troops, castle, and courage.

How vain.

And Ever Thanks
Diana Woodcock

All around me people complaining,
moaning about our year-long
predicament, and though I know
it's a tragedy—so many lives
and livelihoods lost, the cost
of COVID-19 obscene,
the words of Shakespeare in
Twelfth Night echo in my mind,
  I can no other answer make
  but thanks, / And thanks,
  and ever thanks.

Thanks that I'm still alive
to take it all in stride. Thanks
for each breath I take, each
ramble I make along the corniche.

Thanks for what social distancing
can teach. Thanks for the light
returning, for spring about to bring

all her gifts, for eyes to see so clearly
the school of fish feeding in warming
bay waters. Thanks for giving me
birds and cats and one Yellow-bellied
House Gecko for companions,
for opening my ears to hear as
the bamboo stalks talk to one another,
and the gentle waves murmur
at the shoreline. Thanks for slowing
me down, turning me around to
look again and see as if
for the first time, to sniff
the fishy petunia-scented air.

Thanks that I go on singing
and clinging *like a limpet*
to a rock, to my one anchor,[2]
that I am nourished by and
flourish in deep silence and
solitude, for the ease in which
I work happily in peace,
that I'm never lonely or lost
for ideas and things to do.

Thanks for the power of prayer
and the knowing that the Giver
is always there. Thanks
for sweeping me up to leap
into love, for all the times of
keeping still enough to observe

---

[2] Virginia Woolfe

climbing vines. Thanks for times
of joy in the midst of grieving
(hard to believe but true),
for the body's persistent will
to exist. Thanks and
ever thanks for bliss.

Photograph - D Ferrara

deaR aunT sydellE
Burt Rashbaum

deaR aunT sydellE,

i know life is backwards it's like living in a salvador dali painting
everything is melting i'm late an ingrate hated debated amongst
piles of whatever Life is piles of newspapers letters books clothing
dust shoes masks tasks undone friends unwon aunts unwritten
love unsmitten heirlooms shattered in fits of anger and screaming
so only tiny shards of glass await max's grandchildren to wonder
what these little tiny bits of whatever have no story no glory no
spring as covid winter undoes sanity lists torn up days have no
names only I am to blame I usually forget my name staring into the
mirror barely recognizing the weirded bearded old man staring
back at me taunting teasing the dead come to me and speak to me
I've seen and been with grandma and grandpa one time it was
uncle aaron actually in my head telling me why not come on over
we're all here this sphere is just blindly orbiting a dying sun no
wonder you haven't heard from me I haven't heard from me there
is only sickness and death but days have no names anymore it's all
one day it's all one month there's light there's darkness there's
sleep there's dreams keeping me awake there's awakening

keeping me dreaming there's no end to this that I can see but tasks erupt masks hide the rest it's just one more test as I egest this syllabic digression compound my own depression can't sit still zone out lose clout shift and shout inside the skull the dome the walls of this home are closing in dosing me in sound and fury a mound of curry can't alleviate the hunger for humans the forgotten rotten hordes the now nameless shameless untamed forlorn barely born torn shreds of personality that is knowing how low I can go into this ditch this rut this greyness of absence of color this unlikely abeyance of dolor this one long day that has lasted from moon to moon the least of me the last of me the past of me relived ungiven unproven unwoven like a scarf unfettered defeated kneed pleading for some change some upchuck of bad luck some iteration of any consternation this lapse in letters this half-blasted unbettering of my half that can still get up to greet the gray to try and remember what it was we all did pre-covid who we all were before the score was untied from the mooring of the boring and the sins of this son unwon unforgiven unriven and deprived of any gathering no horizon on the horizon no more questions requiring answers too much tv zoning out on blank walls endless snow and wind cutting into conversation shutting out the light the deprivation of want the unknown peace there's no release as time is cruel and the calendar is a collection of mysterious pages with no meaning no gleaning deciphering the sad runes of a nameless day as words pour out into a void of unknowing ungoing surrounded by walls that define the twine that binds me to noW.

Inauguration Day, 2021
Paul Telles

After a week of pounding rain,
I get one clear, cool day

To rake the festering leaves
Off the slope of my yard.

The tines pass easily through
The dry upper layer, but hang

And tangle in the sodden mass
Below. I claim the job is done

When I've exposed the moss,
The mud, the starving grass

Now basking in the winter light.

Aftermath
Paul Telles

When the flood recedes,
The raccoons, the squirrels,
And the tiny starving birds
Emerge like kids after
Their parents fight, skittering
Past shattered shotglasses,
Sniffing air filled with the tang
Of half-smoked cigarettes
Laying their ashes on the table.
The animals and the kids
All hear a silence so loud
It drowns out the stream
And the murmurs behind
The adults' Big Closed Door
And even the thumping static
Of a radio stuck between stations.
The animals have seeds to peck,
Nuts to hoard, nests and trash
To raid. The kids have
This question: Which hurts more,
The silence or the shouting?

Gut Reaction
Paul Telles

Why don't you just lie here and listen
While morning pulls itself together
Outside your window? Voices push their kids
To play. Cars roar. The distant thud
Of a pile driver founds more office space.

Your friends are all off at rallies for peace
And quiet. Do you remember how,
In high school, your protractor shattered
When you tried working all the angles?
Why get up now to face the curvy women
Who smirk at you in checkout lines?
Why tease your twelve remaining hairs
And count the years you didn't live?

You claim disaster spells out all the truth
You need, so you know nothing really helps
When waking shows you the wreck of your marriage
For months on end. Ain't it funny
How despair tastes like Diet Coke?

Would your old girlfriends still date you?
Is the rain cruel enough to fall all day?
You need to change. You hug your belly.

Photograph - Jeff Talarigo

Election Day 2020
Dotty LeMieux

In climates where the
temperatures rarely, if ever, drop
below 50°F, the honeybee colony
keeps working all year-round.
Encyclopedia Britannica

This is the day I cut my own toe attempting
a clumsy pedicure at the edge of the tub, then
tumble backward, bashing a rib
into the edge of my fickle scale

my husband locks himself out of the office, calls
impatient—*you don't answer your phone*
I'm down on my knees, bloodied
thinking about breathing in
and breathing out

How deep is the breath
in this old battered body?
No spring in this chicken
and the hair, uncombed, frantic

Bone, muscle gristle, what
is being born today is not me
or you, maybe a nation, or a notion
of decency after all, maybe a chance
to dream

Ribs will heal, skin be restored
with Neosporin and a band-aid
keys delivered
But what of our Republic?
What of hope?

Will they wither and fade
like last season's tomato plants?
Or blossom like a winter rose, translucent,
still attractive to life-sustaining bees
who beat all odds by resolute
pumping of wings
to fly?

Like It Was Normal
Dotty LeMieux

On a Sunday night we go next door
to say goodbye to the neighbors moving
across the country

Like it was normal, we go
right inside the house
to share farewells

Like it was normal, a small
group has gathered
wearing masks and touching nothing

Suddenly the one leaving
grabs me in a hug
I want to hug back

like it was normal, but freeze,
stiffen against rudeness
to protect myself, her,

the one leaving to care
for her newly widowed father
and the neighbors staying behind

the ones we see everyday
on dog walks, getting the mail, passing
never closer than six feet

Goodbyes are quick, we promise
emails, phone calls, run
back home, embarrassed

Like it was normal, we lock
the door behind us, wash
our hands for twenty long seconds

take our temperature for 10, 14 days
scour each other and the web
for unusual symptoms

put up talismans to ward off
evil spirits
like it was normal.

What Happens to Me Happens Also to You
Dotty LeMieux

Never more apparent than in a pandemic

I reach for the door of the refrigerated case
in the supermarket and you reach for it too
Our hands meet, but only on cold steel
What I deposit there, you receive and carry
and pass on to the next item in the store
and your car and then take home
to your children

What you deposit, I pick up and carry
to the lettuce, the spinach, the Winesap apples
I reject as unripe
and home to rest on the doorknob
and the back of my husband's neck

Even with a mask, with washing, with taking
no chances, I become you and you become me
We are mirror images of each other
even in the best of times

The multitudes within me are within you
They grow and multiply and so enlarge us
until there are no distinctions made
no boundaries formed,
no alliances claimed, shored up,
fought for

When even the dogs in their ignorance
join the chain of becoming infected
with us,
their eyes pleading
for touches
for treats
for any small reassurances
of consistency and love.

Weight of Being...
R.F. Mechelke

I can't remember the turns and stops that brought me home. I remember my hands feeling like stone while gripping the steering wheel and my body feeling pressed down, gasping for breath. I have had these days before. Therapy has helped me recognize the signs. My husband thinks if I know what's happening, I should be able to push it away, to be myself again. All I can say to him is it's like fear, sometimes you can overcome it, but you can never escape it, and most often, all I can do is curl up, and wait for it to pass. The depressive mood of anxiety attacks are paralyzing.

So I stare at the droplets of rain as they streak without care and purpose, driven by the invisible force of gravity, down the large window, a portal to a jungle pretending to be a garden, much like my life. My eyes follow several drops across the weeping glass, choosing a possible victor for the race to the bottom. The air flows across my bare arms, stinging like the shock of cold water after falling through ice. I pull my knees up, slouching back into the deep sofa. My drop loses, and I console myself by pulling a blanket over my arms and chest.

After I pour a glass of wine, I turn on my music. Steve is always trying to change it, without understanding. Sad music has an uplifting effect on me many people just shake their heads at. It's addicting. I can't explain when asked. Why do I need to? I accept it, so should they. The truth is, I don't know why the sound of Sarah McLachlan's lyrics and notes dance in my head, touching off waves of dopamine that feel like warm fingers kneading me to wake, sparking my limbs to move to finish the day with hopefully enough strength to get out of bed tomorrow, to repeat it all again and again. Perhaps it is a shared loneliness that makes me feel as though there is someone out there who understands. So much so, they are able to articulate it with a perfect string of notes and chords and matching lyrics. Or maybe the music just focuses my brain in a way I need to drown out the dark thoughts of paranoia, the thoughts that make me believe without a doubt that I will be fired tomorrow from my job of ten years, pieced together through insights only I can see. For many years, before therapy opened my eyes to what was really happening, I thought I had an intuitive sense akin to a clairvoyant, like the time I knew my husband was cheating. I was so horribly wrong. He had whispered in my ear as we sat on this very sofa, close and sweating from a long fight, that he loved me, that I was the only one for him. Steve was the one who suggested therapy, and it was Dr. Goodall who recognized what was happening to me. I am relieved to know. But relief is fleeting. And I go on, fighting my way through each day, exhausted, and as I lie next to my husband, I wish to be just a little bit normal. Yes, a little bit would be enough.

Not Lonely Alone
Vivian Imperiale

In March my doctor told me
to stay inside "for the duration."
I am complying to save my life.
But staying in is not as isolating
as people may suppose.

I am noticing more—
the variety of birds of all sizes
who visit me in the garden,
coming closer than ever
so we look into one another's eyes,
connecting for the moment.
The flowers pay no heed
to the drought or bad air
and reach farther up toward me
than ever before.

I leave water in the birdbaths
and wonder in the morning,
what other critters drank it up,

waiting for me to replenish the pools.
I suspect raccoons.

And then there are the internal discoveries,
journeys I had little time to take before.
I travel inside myself and roam around
and find those trips interesting.
I retrieve memories and gain insight
into how I got to who I am.

There is time for writing to process
what is in me and what is outside me.
So much these days.
And, when I share, friends are grateful for
"...helping me deal with emotions
I didn't even know I had."

And, most of all,
I have given myself permission
to live each day
without the pressure of "I should."

Loss In Seven Parts
Jennifer Judge

I. Spring: Last Snowfall

Onion snow falls on a Sunday afternoon,
flakes of mica that live and die in a single breath.
The neighbor calls out across the yard,
Time to plant the onions.
Instead my husband plants seeds that will not grow,
elusive things, twenty months and still nothing grows.

II. Memory: First Kiss

The stubble of his face,
always rough, each kiss a kind of damage.
Blue star blanket, a night sky
spread across the floor,
cotton cool and dense against my bare thighs.
The feeling of this first kiss—
wrong, overwhelming—
too much mouth and too
little tongue, a feeling

like not breathing, like
being separated from earth,
outside of time.
We'll say it is summer.

The years pass in a blur.

III. Infertility History

Office of a specialist
smells like piss, forms
filled out in triplicate,
and rubbing alcohol.

No tears.
This is a place for people without hope
or for those who cling to it desperately.

Too many bills,
it stops here,
the falling stops.
We find an end to grief,
the bottom we can touch.
Out of control and then just over.
That's it, over.

IV. Mourning

Mourn the passing of another month
and the flakes of snow falling.
Mourn the small pang of pain, an egg
slipping out into nothingness,

Mourn the blood, deeper,
redder each month,
a loss, a loss, a loss.

V. Costs

Days are a circular blade
dividing us in two—
the blade must take part of us,
just the cost of each pass.

VI. Anger

It seeps through daily interactions
like water soaking into concrete,
a cartoon evil that grows and grows,
this blackened part inside.
It is a person that sits between us
on the couch, that sleeps in our bed
pushing us with its feet and arms to separate us.

VII. Fall

This year I notice the smell of leaves
all the time, that sweet brown decay.
I want to roll in them, make love in the
crush and crackle of it, in the orange
and red and gold of it until
I can't breathe from the straining.
I want to believe in the possibility
of earth to create life, of the trees
to produce new hard buds

and green again; I want to believe
in bodies that contain the possibility
of life, whole and functioning again,
the life that surges forward in a rush
and crackle, the swirl of yellow leaves
kicked up in the wind at the end
of my street so beautiful that I had to
stop the car to catch my breath.

Brave New World
Jennifer Judge

Brave new world, I say,
taking your hand,
blinking back
tears as we cross the parking
lot of a Home Depot.
We will look at lamps, buy
something new.

We have just packed your office,
spent the afternoon wandering
around dusty rooms where
computers still whir with life
though all inhabitants have
departed this building.

A company goes out of business:
Shelves empty, conveyer
belts still, lifeless mannequins
tip over on dirty wood floors,
windows smash
or accumulate grimy soot.

We have said goodbye
to the life you used to have—
steady salary, corner office,
a clear sense of purpose.
We don't know what
the future will bring.

You squeeze back, say,
Aldous Huxley,
I want to get that book.

Married Battles
Jennifer Judge

Yesterday was all hardness and loss,
the rain, infertility, sorrow at our differences,
but night makes us want to give in,
early darkness and the long hours alone.

He turns on our favorite old TV show,
reminds me he is not the enemy.
The show is about tenderness, differences—the dumb
blonde and the lawyer-farmer, softness and the resolve.

She tells him that he doesn't love her,
asks him to write poems to prove it,
and doesn't know that he doesn't write them.
He will convince her again and again.

I remember lost afternoons of last spring,
another house project, both of us exhausted by effort.
But eventually the ceiling repaired, a paint brush
dipped in lavender spread a canopy of tenderness above us.

There is too much to say, too much to grieve,
we hold back, hold back, hang onto this,
regret is too hard to live with
and we only have each other.

Positively Dreadful
Allan Lake

On a mission, coronavirus pioneers
to plenteous anthrosphere to share
its simple message, which hosts
ignore at everyone's peril.
Creator is alive and still creating.
Dread virus prunes one rogue species,
culling weakest until tardy vac-payback.
Pets unaffected. Air pollution down
as shares yo-yo. Chaos in markets but
silence at shopping malls. A chilling
order imposed. Chance to reset the civil
in civilisation now that we have unwittingly
entered an arranged marriage for better
or worse with a clear shortage of better.
Probably high time when Money sails
to islands that barely exist because
it might have to cough up for schools
and hospitals. Pitiless little virus.
So much like us! Wants to go forth
and multiply. It can't be all bad.

As It Is - David Michael Jackson

This Hue of Sky Taps
Mario Duarte

across the trillions of snow
        diamonds, with skin-cracked
knuckles, and pinkish
        fingernails, and gray eyelashes

until the soles of the sun
        step across your feet
despite the 8 degrees,
        enter open pores,

like water through stone,
        inch by inch light climbs
up ankle, thigh, stomach,
        rolls around the ribs,

tickles the clavicle, fine
        notes, and bocce ball
roll to whistle up
        your throat, barely

avoiding the parted lips,
        a forehead rub
before the geyser
        explosion out of

your crown, ah yes,
        a return to hue,
to petals of the sun,
        no stalk, just light.

hope is not in spite of
Russell Willis

hope is not in spite of
not because we are unsure
not hyper-doubt or baseless guess
not blindness to what lies ahead
but expectation of not-yet come
expectation not yet planned
but nonetheless expected

not hope against hope
but that upon which to forge a life
the strength to make it so
the step beyond the step just taken
to know this breath is not the last
this fear does not define

the question begged
not were we right to hope, but
where will this hope lead?

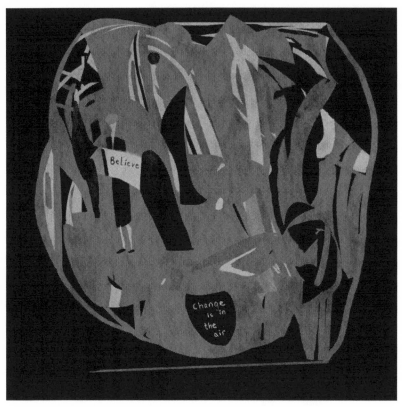

Believe: Change is in the Air - Deb Hemley

Bookends
Shelly Gill Murray

The hardest thing about a pandemic is the feeling of living in between time. It's the days of Lent without the reward at the end; you ate the chocolate bunny just to get through the first day of "shelter in place." I have been here before.

In 1998, 1999 and 2000, my husband and I lived in Bogotà, Colombia, for five weeks each time, waiting for our children's adoption papers to be processed by the Colombian courts. Knowing when the coronavirus pandemic will end is like knowing when the Colombian judge will sign the adoption decree. "*Mañana, en la mañana.*" In the morning, tomorrow, crushing our spirits daily the way the governor's weekly coronavirus updates do.

Like bookends, life with my children began with a "shelter in place" in Bogotà and will end the same way as our youngest heads off to college in the spring. Survival during this time looks both different and the same in 1998 Colombia and 2020 Minneapolis.

In 1998, my husband and I had been married only two years and were just starting our careers in public accounting and law. We were used to working 80 hours a week with no one but ourselves to care for in a three-bedroom home. In Bogotà, we lived in a *pensione*, which, unlike its romantic Italian cousin, was a cross between Airbnb and a youth hostel. The house we stayed in was owned by a dentist and had five bedrooms and bathrooms, a shared living room and dining room, and a small courtyard in the back. Our housemates, ten adults, five soon-to-be adopted infants and three toddlers, were from Sweden, Germany, and France.

Although never quiet, we spent a lot of time in our bedroom because it provided our only personal space. We had twin beds pushed together. Even with all the bedding tucked tight on the corners, the old mattresses looked and felt lumpy. The room had a view of the mountains sliced up by metal grates covering the wall of windows. The second wall consisted of a built-in wardrobe, desk and chair, and a pink puffy old lounge chair with broken springs. Placed in the corner a canvas box crib like those in the bulkhead of a plane was fastened to a wooden frame with crossed legs similar to a hotel luggage rack. While the room was rather large, it lacked any comfortable furniture, so we often sat on the bed or the floor.

We were vulnerable with our limited ability to speak and read Spanish. On average, each day, seven Americans were kidnapped for ransom in Bogotà, deemed one of the top no travel zones by the Department of State. Our attorney and interpreter gave us permission to walk to the mall a few blocks away to shop, but all other outings had to be in a car accompanied by a Colombian. Our world became a four-block box with no computers, and a single shared phone on which to call home cost more than we could afford. Without an easy way to communicate with our workplaces, we were fortunate to be given an unearned leave from our jobs to complete the adoption.

The house was fully staffed so we did not have to cook or clean. We were served three full hot meals and day. Breakfast included a weak cup of instant Nescafè, since all the best coffee was exported to the United States. Out of boredom, we visited the mall for coffee and dessert or to develop photos of us doing nothing to send nowhere. We'd stop by the bank for cash where there was always a line because mail service was so limited, Colombians paid their bills in person. An armed guard effortlessly separated people in line with a gesture from the tip of his machine gun.

Our world was turned upside down, but there were two things that worked in our favor. First, some streets were closed on Sundays to allow families to exercise. We could participate because the crowds were full of parents and children. Second, Bogotá is at an elevation of 8,600 feet whether it was the smog or altitude, we had trouble breathing and we seemed to burn more calories moving about, which counter-balanced our bored and nervous overeating. While a wonderful opportunity to spend time bonding with our children and each other, it was a hell of a lot of time with little to do.

Which brings me back to life in the time of a pandemic. Physical safety is again at stake. I don't know how the odds compare between kidnappings in Bogotá and the virus in Minneapolis. They are both scary, put us on edge, and limit our freedom.

In March when the Governor called for shelter in place, my husband took over the dining room as his office and is now working long hours trying to guess where the economy is going. Our travel and entertainment costs dipped to zero, but our grocery bills tripled. Unlike our time in Colombia when we had almost no communication with others who share our language and culture, we live now in a non-stop online world, where there is no escape because everyone is a free Zoom call away. Physically separated, we have transitioned to consuming media at a pace equal to our calorie intake, but it isn't nourishing us. Luckily, the parkways in

Minneapolis are closed to traffic and more people can exercise at a safe distance. To come down from the overconsumption of food and media, we might need to move to a Wi-Fi-free higher elevation.

No longer babies in Colombia demanding every minute of our time, my adult children don't need me much anymore. They seem like foreigners at times with their limited communication while stuck at home without their friends and too many rules. Looking back, I am not sure who is easier to live with—European strangers who reluctantly agreed to speak English after chastising lazy Americans for failing to learn other languages, or my bilked college kids who rarely speak to me at all.

As the virus reminds us, the between time, like Lent, proposes, even demands, a death of old our ways and invites us to a new way of living. Until then, there are moments that can only be shared in this quiet time of being together, of just being. In Bogotà, I remember the first time my daughter turned at the sound of my voice and recognized me as her mother. In Minneapolis, I text my adult children to come down from their rooms when dinner is ready, and they do come to the table. We eat together as a family again, a ritual I can only count on a few times a year going forward. It's enough for now.

The rest we leave to *la mañana*.

Around the Bend
Elizabeth Nash

Swerving curves
On a road without end
Quiet the nerves
Transcend
Read the signs
The turn is tight
Don't cross lines
Catch the light
Taking a toll
Hands on the wheel
Regain control
Notice how I feel
What I think about
Rest stop
Breathe in, breathe out
Dodge the cop
In overdrive
As rain pours down
I arrive
In another town

Step on the brake
Recover, mend
Don't break—
Come around, bend.

My Left Eye's No Good
Craig Czury

up close, but with my right eye I can see you reading this. I have an acute sense of hearing because of this, relying on what others say about what I should have read or have been reading with both eyes. The words on the page are sliding into and out of each other. But, that's not my problem. My problem is the sea. The ocean with its waves, and me, my Pisces, naturally drawn into it...when you see pants and shirt on the beach...I don't need to finish these sentences, you already know me. But, you don't know me without my glasses when the waves are breaking. With my right eye, they're breaking way out there and I'm cool with wading out to meet them. But, with my left eye, I immediately duck under or shoulder crash into or get knocked over. There's no fuckin' way I'm going to survive this with both eyes open. From either side of this wave, I'm a cyclops.

I'm In A Taxi
Craig Czury

with Giannis Ritsos. He's driving, using Kazantzakis GPS. We're taking the shortcut. Miles from any pavement, scrubby vine grapes pistachio trees. We left the dirt road back at the goats and now straddling a spatter of sun-bleached stones. When we catch a glimpse of the Aegean he says we'll cut the pie under the water. I don't know what that means, but I say ok, as the teeth the statue of Poseidon in the olive grove begin to swivel. He's going to rig it so I get the coin. Because we're twins, he'll get the coin too. In Mexico, it's a plastic baby Jesus inside the cake. What do I know. This is poetry and I have to rely on ambiguity as good as you, but I know you don't. I'm trying to get to the airport in Athens and this is the shortcut. I have 3 days before my flight and I'm running late.

a possibly real apocalypse
Cynthia Hilts

were you ever afraid the people you
dreaded most in junior high were going to
be the boss of you forever but you got sexy
and fashionable all of a sudden
when the glasses and braces came off and as
a consequence with some inherited family traits drank
yourself not quite to death and
by pure luck lived through a self-induced
apocalypse only to rise up and dive down for thirty
years or so until you reached a possibly real apocalypse
in which all your half-ass plans to escape the crushing
idiocy of a country dedicated to dumbing down
and reactionary false dichotomies
and maintaining an impossible status quo
with built in slavery and very
attractive cosmetic self-abuse,
all your half-ass plans to escape became moot
in the inconceivably perverse higher power's
plan for a real new world order with a side of plague
or was it a good old-fashioned global

plague with a side of dictatorship by
who else other than a bastion of old white
thieving murderous psycho clowns and
their ignorance-encrusted flock of patriyokels?
were you?

Reading in the Current Crises
Tara Menon

Amidst the increasing death counts
that turn my lips downward
when I listen to the news in the morning,
while vapor from my coffee rises,
I keep a grateful mental diary—
my husband's safely retired, my son's content
he doesn't have to waste time commuting
behind a procession of honking cars in Boston's notorious traffic,
albeit thinned now as the tentacles of the coronavirus grip
even the invincible young,
time for me expands
to accommodate my writing and reading that once
revolved around household chores,
plus the duties of a mother, a daughter, a wife.
I participate in a Black Lives Matter protest
and pen two tribute poems to George Floyd.
Tears are the ink of a poet,
I learn from Julia Alvarez's *In the Name of Salomé*.
The novel brings alive the eponymous heroine
from the Dominican Republic.

devour Isabel Allende's *A Long Petal of the Sea*,
Laila Lalami's *Conditional Citizens*
and feel like gifting these radiant gems to the president,
but the blind will not see immigrants in a new light.
Miraculously a fresh friendship,
grown in literary soil, sprouts for me,
and I recommend Suketu Mehta's *This Land is Our Land*,
and she passes the baton on.
Can anyone read this memoir
and not cheer on immigrants struggling to forge new paths?

Photograph - D Ferrara

Conversation with a Little Stone Angel During the Trump Presidency
Tara Menon

Little stone angel under the tree,
in the waning light, what do you see?
Little angel, please don't weep.
I need you to be brave because I'm weak.
Do you wish you had a flesh and blood face?
Do you yearn to be in a safer place?
Are you disappointed with the world today?
Has it long passed its heyday?

Your soft voice cuts through the wind,
brushing away the worries of my mind.
Thank you for that insight.
Now I can survive the cold night.

Alternate Reality
Tara Menon

What do we do when villains are lionized as heroes?
Do we remember *The Emperor without Clothes?*
Should we stand by when flatterers kowtow
or should we bellow out the truth
through the media and social platforms?
Can we flush them out of power
or do we tolerate their lies and misdeeds
and megalomaniac behavior?
Are we to remain passive while our children
grow up in an alternate reality?
What will happen to the world
when villains are hailed as heroes
and heroes are depicted as villains?

When true villains are knocked off their pedestals
we applaud, we cheer, we feel justice has finally prevailed
after we waited so long for this reckoning.

Triptych
Burt Rashbaum

1.Outside My Window

This fatigue a
weakness
sheathed in fever

I barely
lift my head
the pillow damp
with sickness

it's all I can
do
to listen to
- need to hear -
human interaction

to bring my eyes
to glass and
take in the social

distancing of

neighbors outside
my window

children playing
      on bicycles
a guitar strumming
      in sun
a lazy old dog
   barks
complaining
      to no one

a car inches
    down the street
its driver masked
      tasked
with a hunt for TP
   or bread instead

a chorus of laughter
    indistinct chatter

of real conversations
    questions   answers
      something funny said
as I exhausted
    exiled isolated

fall back
to bed.

2. 8 PM

every night at 8
as
the curtain of dark
begins its spring
descent to erase
the day

our town cheers.
Like yours, at 7.

Barely able to lift
my head
I lie, apillowed
and listen to the
cheering, hooting, screaming,
drowning out the
rushing creek oblivious, vicious
with snowmelt.

I want to cry out,
I will join you!
When my strength
returns!
I am here,
hearing you!

But, still invisible,
I can only
take in
my town's rowdy

noise.
My sick salty tears
are no more adding
to our celebration
of all those
keeping us alive, fed, cared
for, than the anonymous
glass of my window.

When, finally, I can
join, and stand
by my open pane,
my voice barely
carries the sound
of my joy, so
instead I blow my shofar,
exuberant and victorious
echoing off the distant
hills, as
a sudden silence
is the response

the revelers unsure of
this sonorous explosion

until I blow again
and am answered
with cheers of
victory,
courage,
invitation,
support, an

almost
innate knowledge
    that here,
somewhere,
        out there,
is one of us

returned
to the world.

3. Coda

Now I join
    the chorus at eight

Now no masks are
    worn in this house

Now if I am asked
    a question, I can
answer in the same room

Now I see the
    grapevine greening,
clematis buds, hints
    of lettuce.

Now the thermometer
    is put away
with the Tylenol.

Still a serial killer
   is at large
speaking 100 languages

convincing some there is
   no danger, come on
out and play

still so many will
   die, so many,
too many, mourned
   by we the survivors,

we the immune,
   and we the
vulnerable uninfected

still afraid to venture
   out, so unsure
in this still new century.

No one knows when
   this will end, nor
how we will emerge,

but all the lies from
   the top down,
the subtle manipulations

of a populace not
   so subtle anymore.
No one knows

what awaits tomorrow,
   what is normal
or what is safe.

And yet, the sky has
   never shone so blue,
human touch remains

our elusive Holy Grail,
   our want, our desire
and endless need

still out of reach
   just six feet away
as the human face

and human race
   has been reduced
to searching eyes

and, no surprise,
   suspicion, or doubt,
or desperation

as the serial killer
   still stalks us,
still free, hungry,

haunted, hunted
and unsatisfied.

Amanecer - Ana M. Tamayo

New Day Dawn/ El amanecer
Ana M. Fores Tamayo

The windchimes quelled with leaden silence.
The stars shone glory in their predawn dusk.
My footsteps rustled, crunched the tumbled leaves
briskly crackling beneath the overhanging eaves.
The wolf dog sniffed the stillborn air,
searching for his morning prey.
Of course he knew he had no chance of darting past,
pouncing on that rabbit ambling o'er the trellis fast,
or the squirrel scampering up the tree limb.
The quiet of the morning air lay thick as fog descending
yet soon the sun would break its silent inkwell,
would streak its loveliness in streams of joy and warmth,
reminding me that even when years' toil is heavy plight,
these morning walks are miracles that flaunt a new day's flight.

El Amanecer
Ana M. Fores Tamayo

An interpretation, not a translation
(because translation is never poetry)

Las campanillas de viento sofocan el silencio brusco.
Las estrellas brillan su gloria en el crepúsculo antes del amanecer.
Mis pasos retumban, crujen las hojuelas caídas,
desmoronándolas bajo los aleros colgantes.
El perro lobo olfatea el aire muerto,
buscando su presa matutina.
Por supuesto sabía que no tenía chance de fugarse,
abalanzándose sobre el conejo que ronda por el enrejado,
o la ardilla que corretea por la rama del árbol.
El silencio que sopla en la mañana se espesa como la amenorada niebla
pero pronto el sol despertará su tintero silencioso,
Lucirá su belleza en corrientes de gozo y calidez,
recordándome que cuando los años son difíciles,
Estos paseos de madrugada son milagros alardeando la primera luz.

The Life of Things
Al Simmons

According to science the universe was an accident,
a mistake, an explosion in the kitchen that went
bang, an unexpected calamity. God was
cooking chowder and the phone rang.
His mother called needing a favor,
one thing led to another,
and the whole house burned down.

So, that's where's God's been, planning
the rebuilding, ordering supplies, thinking
about the future while we're left with the cosmic rubble,
toxic background radiation, fires lighting up
the night sky for so long we think it's normal.

God went AWOL with the universe on fire,
and the fire is expanding
faster than the speed of light.

Black holes sweep the sky like robot vacuum cleaners,
but they can't keep up. They do the best they can
sucking up the muck.

Then mankind arrived. He may not be perfect, but
before man there were no written laws, at all. Most
early arrivals perished from disease, incest, violence,
or starved to death.

But for the most part
things are better today, for humans, at least.

Indoor plumbing has been a godsend.
Then came electricity, and appliances.

We're hoping sooner or later, God will get his house in order.
But, these plagues are God's work, according
to scripture. He alone can bring plagues.
Not bats.

I'm surprised no one points that out.

American Tragedy
Candice Kelsey

The chorus of slave women
tossed from their throats
a wish to reverse all the rivers
unwind their Corinth
like Medea's smoky braids

like the month I left Chicago
setting up home in L.A.
days after the '94 earthquake
seeing the La Cienega exit ramp
a crumbled concrete oracle

reminder that freeways are feathers
home is potion and myth
songs are steel blades we choose
and *rivers never reverse*
but the ground—it can shift

as easily as the U.S. Capitol
on the 6th of January 2021
becoming a swarm of chants and shards
with riot gear and rifles
mad torrent of revenge collapsed

Photograph - David R. Brubaker

Circê in Texas
Candice Kelsey

for Atatiana Jefferson, murdered in her
home on October 12, 2019

They bring their own wands
blue extensions of hands
brutal and boyish bands
to rape Edenic lands
their body cams
find the entrance to my cottage
and see what stands

behind a siren song
not for right but wrong
not for Odysseus
or even Ulysses
but for the law for Fort Worth:

This is the police.

They think sending scouts
to figure my smoky cottage out
will end with no account
they soon found out
you'll all find out

as you swine out
at the tip of *my* wand
my hand magic feminine band—

Helios birthed me with light
Persê with water
and my sisters with magic
to see swine for swine
to say *no more* letting men
out their pen out of their fen

for bringing brutal wands
body cams
sudden hands to shoot
here and now *yes sir*
by my power too *sir*
like Circê the witch I
send them squealing to their pen.

Down swine, and root!

Paese dei Sogni
Hilary Sideris

dreamland

Let me, make
me sleep, you say

& turn your back
as if I were the one

keeping you up—
lasciami dormire,

fammi sognare—
as if I made you

dream & wake
saying *Oh Dio,*

*ho fatto un brutto
sogno.* In our bed

or through the wall,
I hear you swear

at Roman pigeons
& your estranged son.

Photograph - David R. Brubaker

There Will Be An After
Linda Murphy Marshall

When cabin fever sets in after nearly a year of the coronavirus-induced shutdown, I take a walk around the small man-made lake in my neighborhood to clear my head, escape from the steady drumbeat of gruesome news. I dodge and swerve away from fellow passersby to keep the requisite six feet between us, our moves resembling a strange square-dance choreography.

Patches of decorated blacktop greet me along the way, multi-colored chalk doodles and writing I can't quite decipher, probably a child's handwriting, some of it partially rubbed away by other walkers' footsteps. The flowers and hearts wend their way across the black surface willy-nilly, each letter a different color and size, their message one of optimism. I've seen stories on TV where children are writing such messages on sidewalks, driveways, and pathways; attempts to lift our spirits, the wisest among us often the youngest. But then I see another short message ahead of me on the path, different, this one in plain white chalk, its stark, uniform block letters neatly stretching across the width of the walkway, devoid of colorful flowers or doodles or happy faces. "There Will Be An After," it reads, and I stop in my tracks to absorb the simple, yet profound words. "Thank you," I whisper to myself and to the universe. "Thank you."

Growing up, my mother had the annoying habit of exhorting me to "Count your blessings!" Her chant pierced the singsongy sound of my whining about this, that, or the other thing, yet only made me feel worse. Now, though, largely confined to my home—along with much of the world—I know what she meant and, more and more, I am discovering there are silver linings to be found, if one will only look; blessings to be counted.

I have a (long) list at the ready of all the ways the coronavirus has impacted me: the long-awaited cruise with my husband to celebrate 30 years of marriage, a trip to New York to see a play with him, another trip there to see a musical with my daughter...on and on my pity party goes. But the serendipitous chalk sign is a reminder that, eventually, this will end and that, along the way, there have been unexpected blessings to come out of the pandemic. And not one of them would have happened were it not for the coronavirus.

I miss going to the library. I miss my volunteer work at the Library of Congress. I miss playing tennis, seeing friends, going to restaurants, the mall, the gym, etc. Some days I feel like this nightmare will never end, my thoughts echoing Buzz Lightyear's words in Toy Story when he calls out: "To infinity and beyond!" Some days it feels like this pandemic will last to infinity and beyond. But from now on I'm going to try and remember the simple chalk message written on my neighborhood pathway. I'm going to count the blessings that have unexpectedly arisen despite the pandemic, and have faith that "There Will Be An After."

Our Contributors

Robert Armstrong is a writer from the Hudson Valley in Upstate New York. A former bookseller, he's been published in a local magazine, *Artless and Naked*, as well as in *Mocking Heart Review*, and will be in upcoming issues of *The Golden Walkman*, and *The Paper Dragon*. He's currently working on poetry chapbooks, short stories and a fantasy novel..

Dale Bailes: Having lived in the Los Angeles area for thirty years and moved back home to the South Carolina coast seven years ago, I have experienced the tumult of earthquakes and hurricanes equally. I prefer to deal with hurricanes, as there is usually some advance warning. With earthquakes, no such luck. I have gotten poems out of both events. The hurricane poem is one of two slated for publication in the Columbia SC literary journal, *Fall/Lines*, in October. The earthquake poem is published herewith.

Elizabeth Browne's stories and essays have most recently appeared in *East Street Magazine, Unstuck*, and the *Fish Publishing Anthology*. She holds an MFA from Emerson College in Boston and lives with her family in San Francisco.

David R. Brubaker is the author of *Liberace's Filipino Cousin* (ThingsAsian Press, 2016). He is happiest exploring planet Earth, mindful that time is short. He has worked and studied in various countries, most notably China and the Philippines, and is a graduate of the University of London. He resides in Lititz, Pennsylvania, with his wife Marilyn and their two cats.

Jacalyn Carley: I'm an expat living in Berlin. After a long career as choreographer who choreographed using literature instead of music, I turned to writing and published four books (in German) along with numerous poems in US journals. I had a severe case of COVID-19 and am dealing with long-haul symptoms as well as the itch that I share with all humanity for life to return to some semblance of normal.

Anne Casey is an award-winning Sydney-based Irish poet and writer. A journalist, magazine editor, legal author, and media communications director for 30 years, her work is widely published internationally, ranking in *The Irish Times' Most Read*. Author of the critically acclaimed poetry collections, *where the lost things go* and *out of emptied cups*, she has two books forthcoming in 2021. Anne has won poetry awards in Ireland, the UK, the USA, Canada, Hong Kong, and Australia. She is the recipient of an Australian Government Scholarship for her PhD in Creative Writing at the University of Technology Sydney. anne-casey.com, @1annecasey

D. Chase-Herber is a writer, painter, and factory worker in the shiny part of the Rust Belt.

Poems by **DeWitt Clinton** have appeared in *Lowestoft Chronicle, New Reader Review, The Bezine, The Poet by Day, Verse-Virtual, Poetry Hall, Muddy River Poetry Review, Across the Margin,*

Art + Literature Lab, Art in the Time of COVID-19, One Magazine, Fudoki Magazine, and *New Verse News*; two poetry collections, *At the End of the War*, (Kelsay Books, 2018), and *Is A Rose Press, By a Lake Near a Moon: Fishing with the Chinese Masters*, poetic adaptations of *Kenneth Rexroth's 100 Poems from the Chinese.* He is Professor Emeritus at the University of Wisconsin, and lives in Shorewood, Wisconsin.

Jean Colonomos has published in several poetry journals, including *American Writers Review*, where her poems received honorable mentions. She has been a featured poet in many Southern California libraries. Other publications where her poems have appeared include *Spillway, Post Grad Journal*, and *Project Ventura County Poetry*. Her chapbook is *Art Farm*, published by Finishing Line Press. She is currently a Pushcart Prize nominee. More information on https://jeancolonomos.weebly.com/

Craig Czury's recent book, (*FootHills, Postcards & Ancient Texts 2020*), is a 40-year collection of napkin poems from his whereabouts from Albania to Argentina. *Fifteen Stones* (*NYQ Books,* 2017) a collection of prose poems from Italy, Chile, and spaces between. *Thumb Notes Almanac: Hitchhiking the Marcellus Shale (FootHills, 2016),* is his collection *of* docu-poems from observations and interviews while hitchhiking around his home northeastern Pennsylvania 'fracking' region. Czury lives, teaches, gives lectures & readings, and organizes poetry events in the US, Italy, Albania, and Lithuania. He is a 2020-21 recipient of a Fulbright Scholarship to Chile. craigczury.com

Dawn Denham's work has appeared in *Banstorm, Brevity, Literary Mama,* & *Past Ten, Poets & Writers, Solstice, Waterwheel Review, Zone 3* and is forthcoming from *Dorothy Parker's Ashes.* Her essay "Aleatorik" won the *Solstice Magazine* essay contest and was nominated for a Pushcart Prize. She writes and teaches in north central Mississippi and is completing her first memoir, *The Blue House.*

Leap Frog - D Ferrara

Kari Despain lives in the Kansas City Metro area and is a current MFA candidate in fiction at University of Kansas. She loves writing about the locations she grew out of: the wilds of the southwestern United States, the jungles of Trinidad, and the south-central heartland. Kari was named a *2016 AWP Intro Journals Project* winner in poetry. Her work has been featured in *Watershed Review, Ponder Review, The Windhover,* and *I-70 Review,* among other journals.

Mario Duarte is a graduate of the Iowa Writers' Workshop. His poems and short stories have appeared in *Abstract Elephant, Bilingual/Borderless, Lunch Ticket, Pank, Pilgrimage, The RavensPerch, Rigorous, Sky Island Journal, Storyscape, 2River*

Review, Write Launch and *Typishly.* New work is forthcoming in *Aaduna.*

Patricia Dutt: I have written for many years and published in small literary magazines. I have worked as a science teacher, a science consultant, a grant writer and a landscape estimator while bringing up three children. And I meditate—every single day.

Jo Angela Edwins has published poems in various venues including *Calyx, New South, Whale Road Review*, and *West Trestle Review.* Her chapbook *Play* was published in 2016. She has received awards from *Winning Writers, Poetry Super Highway*, and the *SC Academy of Authors.* She teaches at Francis Marion University in Florence, SC, where she serves as the poet laureate of the Pee Dee region of South Carolina.

Rachel Elam, based in New York City, Rachel Elam's work has been published in *New York Magazine, Beyond Words Literary Review, Las Lagunas Gallery* and more

Rachel Evans is a writer, actress, and high school drama teacher based in Brooklyn. Her one-woman show, *Jew Wish*, premiered in the NY Fringe Festival and was subsequently performed in multiple venues. Her short plays and monologues have had readings or performances at various theaters in NYC. Her essays have appeared on the website Kveller, and in the 2021 book *Sex with Everybody* (Little Brown & Co.), and the anthology *Lyrics, Lit & Liquor.* She dedicates *What I know* to the memory of her beloved aunt, Linda Ehrenfreund, whom she misses every day.

Editor **D Ferrara** has been a writer, editor, and collaborator for more years than she cares to remember. She is honored to be the editor of *American Writers Review* and *Art in the Time of COVID-19*, among other publications.

Gregory Fletcher. "Thanks, Dad—I Think" appeared in *American Writers Review,* Summer 2018 edition. Other essays include "The Unsealed Letter" in the anthology *Being: What Makes a Man* (Univ. of Nebraska-Lincoln); "Dallas Guilt" in the anthology *Dearly Beloved* (Zoetic Press); and "*manhood/'man,hood/noun*" (Longridge Review). Short stories, "Friends of Vera" in the anthology *Night Bazaar,* and "Ismene in Venice" in *Night Bazaar: Venice,* both published by Northampton House Press, who published my YA novel *Other People's Crazy,* and craft book *Shorts and Briefs,* a collection of short plays and brief principles of playwriting. I am a playwright with a dozen off-off-Broadway productions.

Patricia A. Florio, born in Brooklyn, founder of *American Writers Review,* discovering her niche in 2011 at Wilkes University where she received her MFA. She is the co-founder of the Jersey Shore Writers, and recipient of two Norman Mailer scholarships in CFN. The author of *My Two Mothers; Cucina Amelia* and *Puppy in my Pocket, was* a featured *Scene* writer for *The Two River Times.*

Ralph F. Florio, married to Pat Florio for 50 years, worked as husband-wife court reporters in Brooklyn and Newark federal court. Retired in 2017, Ralph now enjoys playing golf. Between holes, he might take a picture of interesting trees.

Ana M. Fores Tamayo: Being an academic not paid enough for my trouble, I wanted to do something that mattered: work with asylum seekers. I advocate for marginalized refugee families from

Mexico and Central America. Working with asylum seekers is heart wrenching yet satisfying; also, quite humbling.

Lara Frankena is a Midwesterner by birth and a Londoner by chance. Her poems have appeared in publications such as *Free State Review, Cream City Review* and *Midwestern Gothic*.

Raising in the slightly different cultures and occasionally uncomprehending cultures of New Jersey, Virginia, England, **Peter David Goodwin** moved back to USA at age 18, in pursuit of an egalitarian education, eventually settling in New York City, working in a variety of occupations while indulging his love for theatre, relishing the City's vibrant chaos, but starved for light, he removed himself to the Chesapeake Bay, appreciating its natural rhythms and slower seasons..

Lenore Hart is author of seven novels, including *Waterwoman, Ordinary Springs, Becky*, and *The Raven's Bride,* and series editor of *The Night Bazaar* fantastic fiction anthologies; most recently *The Night Bazaar: Venice* (August 2020). She's published numerous short works of fiction, nonfiction, and poetry, and received awards, grants, and fellowships from the National Endowment for the Arts, several state arts councils, the Irish Writers Union, and the Oberpfalzer Kunstlerhaus, Germany. She serves on the IWU's executive committee. Hart teaches in the graduate writing program at Wilkes University, and at the Ossabaw Island Writers Retreat, Savannah. She lives in Virginia.

Deb Hemley is a multimedia artist and writer who lives in Massachusetts.

Cynthia Hilts, poet, jazz pianist, vocalist, composer and lyricist, bandleader, and teacher. Her primary values as an artist of any genre, is that blood moves in the body of the art she produces. Her work has been published in *ITWOW* (*In The Words of Womyn*) *Anthology, Carbon Culture, Inwood Indiana Press, 50 Haikus*, and *Poetry Quarterly*. She has recorded four CDs of original music and lyrics.

Richard Holinger's collection of poems, *North of Crivitz*, poems focused on rural Upper Midwest, and *Kangaroo Rabbits and Galvanized Fences*, a collection of humorous essays about domestic life, are available on Amazon or richardholinger.net. He has received four Pushcart Prize nominations. His fiction, poetry, and essays have appeared in *Witness, The Iowa Review, The Southern Review,* and *Boulevard.*

Vivian Imperiale started writing at the age of six. She uses poetry to help her identify and process her feelings about life events. She is retired from the mental health field but her 40+ years of advocacy continue.

David Michael Jackson: An artist, poet, songwriter, musician, engineer, and web publisher, I have published *Artvilla.com* continuously since 1998. We published so many MP3s on the early internet that we became a record label. I also publish *Artvilla's* sister site, *Motherbird.com*, another 1998 site. Who is David Michael Jackson? Someone who has published himself so well that he is a shadow in the night delivering a poem or a painting. Check my songs on Spotify or my poetry with music as *Modern Music Nashville.*

Rosie Johnston, this is my first fiction in ten years. I had two novels published (in Dublin and London) until life intruded and made another (commissioned) novel impossible. Poems came instead and four books of my poetry have been published in my native Belfast. I thought fiction had deserted me until I visited Paris in February last year and had an encounter that sparked this story. It is an attempt to bring together something of what we have been through over this past year, refracted through several kinds of love.

Jennifer Judge teaches creative writing at King's College in Wilkes-Barre, PA. One of her poems was selected for permanent inclusion in the Jenny Holzer installation *For Philadelphia 2018*, appearing in the lobby of the Comcast Technology Center. Her work has appeared in *Literary Mama, Blueline, Under the Gum Tree, The Comstock Review, Gyroscope Review,* and *Rhino,* among others. Her first book, *Spoons, Knives, Checkbooks*, is due out from Propertius Press in summer 2021 She earned an MFA from Goddard College and lives in Dallas, PA with her husband and two daughters.

Babitha Marina Justin is from Kerala, South India. Her poems have appeared in *Eclectica, Esthetic Apostle, Fulcrum, The Scriblerus, Chaleur Magazine, Into the Void, Trampset, Inlandia, The Paragon Press, Adolphus Press, The Punch Magazine, Rise Up Review, Constellations, Cathexis NW Press, Silver Needle Press, About Place Journal, The Write Launch, Trampset, The Four Quarters Magazine, So to Speak journal, Kritya* and *Journal of Post-Colonial Literature.* Her first collection of poetry, *Of Fireflies, Guns and the Hills,* was published by the Writers Workshop in 2015. She is also waiting to debut as a novelist with *Maria's Swamp.*

R. J. Keeler, Carolina State University, MS Computer Science University of North Carolina-Chapel Hill, MBA University of California at Los Angeles, and Certificate in Poetry University of Washington. Honorman in the U.S. Naval Submarine School and Submarine Service (SS) qualified. Recipient of the Vietnam Service Medal, Honorable Discharge, and Whiting Foundation Experimental Grant. Member of IEEE, AAAS, Academy of American Poets. A former Boeing engineer. He has two poetry collections, *Detonation* and *Snowman*, both published in 2020.

Photograph - Jeff Talarigo

Candice Kelsey teaches writing in Los Angeles. Her poetry appears in *Poets Reading the News* and *Poet Lore* among other journals. Her first collection, *Still I am Pushing*, was released last year. She won the 2019 Two Sisters Writing's Contest and was recently nominated for both a Best of the Net and a Pushcart. Find her at www.candicemkelseypoet.com

Richard Key was born in Jacksonville, Florida, and grew up in Mississippi. He now lives in Alabama where he works part-time as a pathologist. His essays and short stories have appeared in a number of literary journals and magazines. His website is: richardkeyauthor.com.

Mila Lachica moved with her family from Panay Island, Philippines, to New Jersey where she currently works as a clinical research coordinator. Her undergraduate folklore research took her around the island collecting riddles. The experience was an inspiring source for writing poetry in her mother tongue, Kinaray-a. Working with a mentor who championed Kinaray-a, not just as a dialect but a language for literary expression, she was awarded a literary grant in poetry and subsequently, playwriting. She remains in touch with other Kinaray-a writers and finds joy in her yard, gardening and taking photos.

Jennifer Lagier has published in a variety of anthologies and literary magazines, taught with California Poets in the Schools, edits the *Monterey Review*, helps coordinate Monterey Bay Poetry Consortium Second Sunday readings. Recent publications: *Harbinger Asylum, The Rockford Review, Syndic Literary Journal, From Everywhere A Little: A Migration Anthology, Fire and Rain: Ecopoetry of California, Missing Persons: Reflections on Dementia, Silent Screams: Poetic Journeys Through Addiction and Recovery.* Newest books: *Camille Mobilizes* (FutureCycle Press), *Trumped Up Election* (Xi Draconis Books), *Dystopia Playlist (*CyberWit*), and Camille Comes Unglued (*CyberWit*).* Forthcoming title: *Meditations on Seascapes* and *Cypress (*Blue Light Press).

Originally from Saskatchewan, **Allan Lake** has lived in Vancouver, Cape Breton, Ibiza, Tasmania, and Melbourne. Poetry

Collection: *Sand in the Sole* (Xlibris, 2014). Lake won Lost Tower Publications (UK) Comp 2017 and Melbourne Spoken Word Poetry Fest 2018, and publication in *New Philosopher 2020*. Chapbook, *My Photos of Sicily (*Ginninderra Press *2020)*.

Sheree La Puma is an award-winning writer whose personal essays, fiction, and poetry have appeared in or are forthcoming in *The Penn Review, American Journal of Poetry, WSQ, Chiron Review, SRPR, The Rumpus, Plainsongs*, and *I-70 Review*, among others. Her poetry was recently nominated for Best of the Net and two Pushcarts. Her micro-chapbook, *The Politics of Love*, was published in August by Ghost City Press. Her new chapbook, *Broken: Do Not Use* was recently released with Main Street Rag Publishing. She received an MFA in Writing from the California Institute of the Arts and taught poetry to former gang members. www.shereelapuma.com

Dawn Leas, author of *A Person Worth Knowing* (Foothills Publishing), *Take Something When You Go,* (Winter Goose Publishing), and *I Know When to Keep Quiet,* (Finishing Line Press). Her work has appeared in *Literary Mama, The Pedestal Magazine, SWWIM, San Pedro River Review,* and elsewhere. She's a writing coach, editor, and teaching artist for Arts in Education NEPA and Pennsylvania Arts in Education Program (PAEP), partner organizations of Pennsylvania Council of the Arts. She's a proud back-of-the-pack runner, newbie hiker, salt-water lover, and mom of two grown sons. Visit www.thehammockwriter.com.

Dotty LeMieux's work has appeared or is forthcoming in publications such as *Rise Up Review, Poets Reading the News, Gyroscope, MacQueen's Quinterly*; anthologies such as the *Marin Poetry Center Anthology*, Moon Shadow, Sanctuary Press'

Enskyment, and others. She has had four chapbooks published, latest from Finishing Line Press entitled *Henceforth I Ask Not Good Fortune*. In the 1980's, she edited the literary magazine *Turkey Buzzard Review*. Her day jobs are running political campaigns, mainly for progressive women, and practicing environmental law in Marin County California, where she lives with her husband and two dogs.

Monique Antonette Lewis is the founder of At The Inkwell. Her fiction and essays have appeared in *My Body, My Words*, *American Writers Review* (Summer 2018), *Polarity eMagazine* (Winter 2017), and *PoetryBay* (Fall/Winter 2016). A former journalist for 14 years, Monique's articles have appeared in *Agence France-Presse*, the *Financial Times, Forbes, HuffPost*, and more. She is currently the MBA Communications Program Manager for HEC Paris and lives in Versailles, France.

Lynnette Li: I am an API actor, early childhood music teacher, writer, and mom, currently living in Chicago.

Carol MacAllister, artist, studied under her internationally known mentors Carmen Cicero and Peter Barnett. Her work has been shown in groups shows at the National Academy of Design. Currently her works are part of the UGA Lyndon House exhibition in Athens, GA.

Linda Murphy Marshall is a multi-linguist and writer with a PhD in Hispanic Languages and Literature, a Master's in Spanish, and an MFA in Creative Writing from Vermont College of Fine Arts. Her nonfiction and fiction work has been published or is forthcoming in *The Catamaran Literary Reader*, *The Los Angeles Review, Maryland Literary Review, Critical Read, American Literary*

Review, Bacopa Literary Review, Adelaide Literary Magazine, Flash Fiction Magazine, Sip Cup, Hobo Camp Review, and elsewhere.

Gale Martin found a constructive outlet for her childhood

penchant of lying, writing creatively since 2005, winning numerous awards for fiction and creative non-fiction. Her most recent work appeared in *My Body, My Words, American Writers Review* (Summer 2018), and her novel, *Polarity was* published by Northampton House. She has a Master's in Creative Writing from Wilkes University and lives in Lancaster County, Pennsylvania.

Photograph - Jeff Talarigo

From her home in Melbourne, **Margaret McCaffrey** is a proud contributor to *American Writers Review* and *Door is A Jar*. More of her stories are published in the Elwood Writers anthology *Every Second Tuesday* (2020) and can be heard on *Cover to Cover*, Vision Australia Radio. In 2011 she received a scholarship to the Norman Mailer Center to develop her memoir. She holds an MA in Creative Writing from Wilkes University. Margaret is currently working on a memoir about her father, Jim, who had been a POW in Germany during World War II.

Helen McDonald is based in country Victoria, Australia, and writes poetry, memoir, and short stories. She is published in Australia and overseas, including *Drifting Sands, a Journal of Haibun and Tanka Prose*, *Creatrix 50# journal*, *American Writers Review* and *Love's Footprint*. She is included in *Democratic Poetry, Poetry Matters 2020*, an anthology of selected poems, 2006—2019. Helen is a member of Elwood Writers and her work is included in their anthology, *Every Second Tuesday*, published December 2020. See elwoodwriters.com

R.F. Mechelke was nominated for *The Best American Mystery and Suspense Stories* series. He holds a BS from Marquette University and a Master's from Cardinal Stritch University. His short stories have appeared in or are forthcoming in the *Blue Lake Review, Loch Raven Review, Sci Phi Journal, Lowestoft Chronicle, MoonPark Review, The Main Street Rag* and elsewhere. Follow him on Twitter @RFMechelke. www.RFMechelke.com.

Tara Menon is an Indian-American writer based in Lexington, Massachusetts. Her most recent poems have appeared in: *Don't Die Press, The Decolonial Passage, Emrys Journal Online, Indolent Books, Wards Literary Magazine, Art in the Time of COVID-19, Rigorous, Infection House, The Inquisitive Eater*, and *The Tiger Moth Review*. Menon's latest fiction has been published in *The Bookends Review, Evening Street Review,* and *Rio Grande Review*. She is also a book reviewer and essayist whose pieces have appeared in many journals, including *Adanna Literary Journal, The Courtship of Winds, The Petigru Review, Boston Globe, Green Mountains Review*, and *The Kenyon Review*.

Mona Miller: I'm a retired lawyer who now concentrates on writing plays, screenplays, and short stories. I grew up in Florida, moved to Manhattan, and then found the wonderful country known as California, courtesy of law school. (Los Angeles satisfied the native Floridian's need for warm weather, sunshine, and the ocean.) I wrote plays and stories starting in childhood but stopped during law school and for the next 11 years. The birth of my daughter triggered a creative renaissance, and I returned to writing.

Shelly Gill Murray is a freelance writer, a former attorney, an ambassador for organ donation, a mission-based world traveler, and jail volunteer. She is a story slam participant on The Moth and her essays can be found in *Gotham Writers*, San Fedele Press e-book *Art in the Time of COVID-19*, *Mn Women's Press*, *Pathways to Children.org*, *Caringbridge.org*, *Adoptive Families Magazine* and *AAA Travel Magazine*.

Lori M. Myers, Award-winning writer and Pushcart Prize nominee of creative nonfiction, fiction, essays, and plays. Master's degree in Creative Writing from Wilkes University.

Elizabeth Nash resides in California. With a BS in Mathematics, she has an intrinsic sense of structure and relationship. She began her 35-year career as a member of NASA's technical staff and ended it combating terrorism for the intelligence agencies. As a child, she was inspired to write about struggle and joy. Influenced by haiku, she developed her style using minimalist phrasing. She is also an artist who has pieces displayed in juried shows. With an open mind, she applies both pen and brush to artistic expression now that she has adopted a more creative lifestyle.

Mary K O'Melveny, a retired labor rights lawyer, lives with

her wife in Woodstock, NY and Washington DC. Mary's work has been nominated for a Pushcart Prize and received other award recognition. Her poetry has appeared in numerous print and on-line journals and anthologies and on national blog sites. She is the author of *Woman of a Certain Age* and *Merging Star Hypotheses* (Finishing Line Press) and co-author of the anthology *An Apple In Her Hand* (Codhill Press). Her

Photograph - Jeff Talarigo

latest collection *Dispatches From the Memory Care Museum* will be published in 2021 by Kelsay Books.

Patrick O'Neil is the author of the memoir *Gun, Needle, Spoon* (Dzanc Books) and *Anarchy At The Circle K*. His writing has appeared in numerous publications, including *Juxtapoz, Salon.com, The Fix, The Nervous Breakdown*, and *Razorcake*. He is a contributing editor for *Sensitive Skin Magazine*, a Pushcart nominee, and a two-time nominee for Best of the Net. With an MFA from Antioch University, he sits on the Board of Directors for REDEEMED, a non-profit criminal record clearing project. O'Neil lives with his wife Jennifer, a Maine Coon, and a squirrel, in Glendale, California. For more information, please visit: patrick-oneil.com.

Michael Penny was born in Australia, but moved to Canada as a teenager. He has published five books, most recently, *Outside, Inside* (McGill-Queen's University Press) and now lives on an island near Vancouver, British Columbia.

Colin Pink's plays have been produced in London, New York City and Berlin. His poems have appeared in *Acumen, American Writers Review, Poetry Ireland Review, Aesthetica* and online at *Ink Sweat and Tears* and *The High Wind.* His stories have appeared in a wide range of literary magazines such as: *High Window.* His first collection of poems, *Acrabats of Sound*, is available from Poetry Salzburg. His second collection *The Ventriloquist Dummy's Lament* has been published by Against the Grain Press.

Anita S. Pulier is a graduate of New York University and New York Law School. After practicing law in New York and New Jersey, Anita served as a U S representative for the Women's International League for Peace and Freedom at the United Nations. Anita's poems have appeared online, in anthologies and in print journals. Her books *Toast* and *The Butcher's Diamond* and her chapbooks *Perfect Diet, The Lovely Mundane*, and *Sounds of Morning* are published by Finishing Line Press.

Poet and writer **A. Rabaduex** is an Ohio native and Air Force veteran who currently lives in Pennsylvania where she teaches college English courses. Her work has appeared or is forthcoming in *Blue River Review, Olney Magazine,* and *Gyroscope Review*, among other journals. She is currently pursuing an MFA in Creative Writing at Wilkes University.

Burt Rashbaum: I've been long published in an array of journals. Last summer, I appeared in *Art In The Time of COVID-19.* Before that my book, *Of the Carousel,* was published by The Poet's Press (Pittsburgh, 2019). I live in Colorado, though born in Brooklyn. Right now, my writing is a lifeline to whatever normal used to be.

Photograph - D Ferrara

Mary Kay Rummel's ninth poetry book, *Nocturnes: Between Flesh and Stone,* has been published by Blue Light Press of San Francisco. Her first book, *This Body She's Entered,* won a Minnesota Voices Award from New Rivers Press. *The Lifeline Trembles* won the Blue Light Award and *Love in the End* was a chapbook award winner from Bright Hill Press. She is co-editor of *Psalms of Cinder & Silt,* poems about experiences with fires in California (Solo Novo Press). The former Poet Laureate of Ventura

County, Mary Kay has read her poems in the US, England and Ireland.

Joel Savishinsky: I am an activist, a writer, and a retired professor of anthropology and gerontology. My most recent book, *Breaking The Watch: The Meanings of Retirement in America,* won the Gerontological Society of America's Kalish Award, its book of the year prize. The places where my poetry, fiction, and nonfiction have appeared, or are in press, include *Beyond Words*, *Blood and Thunder*, *Cirque*, *Down in the Dirt*, *Evening Street Review*, *Metafore*, *The New York Times*, *Passager*, *Right Hand Pointing*, *Soul-Lit, Windfall*, and *Xanadu.*

Hilary Sideris's poems appear in recent issues of *The American Journal of Poetry, Barrow Street, Bellevue Literary Review, Free State Review, Mom Egg Review, Rhino, Room, Salamander, Sixth Finch*, and *Verse Daily*. Her most recent book, *Animals in English*: *Poems after Temple Grandin,* was published by Dos Madres Press in 2020. She is a co-founder of the CUNY Start program, which helps prepare underserved high school graduates from New York City and around the world for credit courses at The City University of New York.

Al Simmons lives in Alameda, California. He has been quoted on the front page of *The New York Times*. Poet-In-Residence, City of Chicago, 1979-80, his work has appeared in *Genre: Urban Arts, Thin Air, Red Coyote, 42 Word Story Anthology, Heron Clan VII, Kanstellation, Illumen, Abyss & Apex*, and *American Writers Review, Art In The Time of COVID-19,* San Fedele Press, *The Martian Wave,* Hiraeth Press, and Clarendon Books *Poetica #2, Inner Circle Writer's Poetry Anthology, 2020.* See more at simmonsink@blogspot.com.

A retired educator, **Dave Sims** now makes art and music in the old mountains of central Pennsylvania. His traditional and digital paintings and comix appear in dozens of tangible and virtual publications, galleries, and exhibits, with new work forthcoming in *Sunspot Literature, Raw Art Review,* and *The Abstract Elephant.* Experience more at www.tincansims.com

Jeff Talarigo is the author of novels *In the Cemetery of the Orange Trees, The Pearl Diver, The Ginseng Hunter,* and numerous short stories. A Pennsylvanian, he has received the American Academy of Arts and Letters Rosenthal Award and a 2005 Kiriyama Prize Notable Book of the American Library Association and was include in NPR's 2008 *Under the Radar.* He has been featured on NPR's Weekend Edition and awarded a Fellowship at the New York Public Library's Cullman Center for Scholars and Writers. His work has been published in five languages. His photography graced *American Writers Review* in 2018, 2019, and 2020.

Crack Up - Holly Tappen

Holly Tappen is often found in her art studio, sweating at the computer while eating Smarties. Influenced by Leonardo da Vinci and Picasso, she will be the world's first Abstract Realist when she figures out what that looks like. Holly has written seven plays and a memoir. Her writing appeared in the book *Jewels of San Fedele*. A million light years ago, she majored in philosophy at Emory University because there was no creative writing program. Although she wants art in every aspect of her life, the IRS does not appreciate this, so she specializes in bad jobs. And has a cat.

Paul Telles's poems have appeared in several online and print publications, including *Book of Matches, Rat's Ass Review, Pif Magazine,* and *BoomerLitMag.*

Butterfly Thomas is the author of the urban thriller *Head Held High* (2018,) *In My Feelings: A Book of Poetry (2020)* and *The Butterfly Effect: A Poetic Call to Action* (2021). She was born in Germany but was raised in Virginia, where she still lives. When Butterfly is not working as a counselor and advocate, she spends her time with the two loves of her life, reading and creative writing. A life-long learner, she tries to watch *Jeopardy!* every night and admits to a hopeless addiction to chocolate.

Barry Lee Thompson: I was born in Liverpool in the UK, and I'm based in Melbourne, Australia. My short fiction is published in Australia, the USA, and the UK. *Broken Rules and Other Stories* (Transit Lounge, September 2020) is my first collection, and is supported by the Victorian Government through Creative Victoria, and by Varuna, the National Writers' House.

Katie Toskaner: I do not take many photos, but quarantining gave me time to pursue new hobbies; however, writing is my usual hobby which I have enjoyed for many years. It leads to another world where one controls destiny—what fun!

Diane Valeri: I am a novice writer living in Bradley Beach, NJ known for its sizzle, drizzle, and frizzle.

Bissera Videnova is a contemporary photographer, poet, writer, and editor in her native tongue. She was born in Sofia, Bulgaria, where she currently resides. At a young age, she participated in movie and television productions. Mrs. Videnova has published both poetry and prose for academic and online articles in her country. In 2012, she won the Mediterranean Women Forum with a short story. Her first poetry collection was published in 2017. She has participated in *Reading Poetry at Royal Poetry Club*, Yale Club Manhattan, and *Reading Poetry at Poets House NYC*.

Lois Perch Villemaire resides in Annapolis, MD. Her stories, memoir flash, and poetry have appeared online and in journals *including Ponder Savant, The Literatus, Trouvaille Review, FewerThan500, The Drabble, Pen In Hand, North of Oxford, Flash Frontier, Flora Fiction* and anthologies published by Truth Serum Press. She blogs for annapolisdiscovered.com..

Julene Waffle is a teacher in a rural public school, an entrepreneur, a wife, a mother of three busy boys, two dogs, three cats, and a fish, and, of course, a writer. Her work has appeared in *La Presa* and *The English Journal,* among other journals, and in the anthologies *Civilization in Crisis* and *Seeing Things*, and her chapbook, *So I Will Remember.* Learn more at www.wafflepoetry.com

Bioethicist and online education entrepreneur, **Russell Willis**, emerged as a poet in 2019. Since then, his poetry has been published (or accepted for publication) in *Intangible Magazine,*

433, Breathe, Peeking Cat, Le Merle, As Above So Below, Grand Little Things, Frost Meadow Review's Pandemic Poetry, October Hill, Cathexis Northwest, Meat for Tea, The MOON magazine, Snapdragon: A Journal of Art & Healing, Tiny Seed Literary Journal, The Esthetic Apostle, and five anthologies. Russell grew up in and around Texas, was vocationally scattered throughout the Southwest and Great Plains for many years, and is now settled in Vermont with his wife, Dawn.

Diana Woodcock is the author of seven chapbooks and three poetry collections, most recently *Tread Softly* (FutureCycle Press, 2018) and *Near the Arctic Circle* (Tiger's Eye Press, 2018). Her forthcoming books are *Facing Aridity* (finalist for the Prism Prize); and *Holy Sparks* (Paraclete Press). Recipient of the Vernice Quebodeaux "Pathways" Poetry Prize for Women for her *Swaying on the Elephant's Shoulders*, her work appeared in *Best New Poets 2008* and has been nominated for Best of the Net and the Pushcart Prize. Currently teaching in Qatar at Virginia Commonwealth University's campus, she holds a PhD in Creative Writing.

Remembering Dr. Arlene Cardinale
Patricia A. Florio

Arlene Cardinale was a woman of many talents, including an ambitious prescience. As a student at Newark's First Avenue Elementary School, she wrote an essay in which she promised to return to the school as its principal. In 1992, she did, on a day she called the happiest of her life.

I met her shortly afterwards, introduced as "Brooklyn Italian" to a "Newark Italian." We laughed, shared a few Neapolitan phrases, and became friends for twenty-two years.

While she never had children, Arlene was the spiritual mother to the children in First Avenue School. They were her pride, joy and, now, legacy. She inspired their educational growth, as she did mine. We will miss her.

Zoom - Patricia A. Florio

You gain strength, courage, and confidence by every experience in which you really stop to look fear in the face. You are able to say to yourself, "I lived through this horror. I can take the next thing that comes along."

Eleanor Roosevelt

Made in the USA
Middletown, DE
27 June 2021